BUILDING KINGDOM CHURCHES

A HANDBOOK FOR WESTERN CHRISTIANS

MARK PERRY

Building Kingdom Churches
Table Of Contents

Acknowledgements

Over the years numerous kingdom people have greatly influenced my thinking and practices as they have faithfully modeled kingdom life and ministry. Every shortcoming in this book is entirely mine and does not reflect on any of these influences. However, I would nonetheless like to acknowledge a few of my heroes who have embodied the paradigms and practices in this book: Rolland and Heidi Baker, John Wimber, Marc Dupont, Steve Witt, Rich Nathan (and numerous others), thank you for modeling kingdom church life the way it should be.

The churches I have been privileged to serve and lead have extended me great grace as I have been working out these paradigms in the laboratory of the local church. We have journeyed and experimented together! Thank you for every bit of it. Thank you to the people of Everyday Church, in particular, who are pressing in to the reality of a community of the kingdom.

Cheryl, thank you for being a model kingdom woman. Audrey, Emily, Olivia, may you continue to embody and express the kingdom, and as Bill Johnson says, may my ceiling become your floor!

Introduction

I love planting and building churches. It has been a study, passion, and practice of mine for some time, and over the past several years I've had the privilege of being involved in the planting and building process repeatedly and from a number of vantage points.

The process of church building is first and best described by our Lord Jesus Christ in Matthew 16:18, where He reveals the foundation and secrets of the building process--

> "Upon this rock I will build My church, and the gates of hell will not prevail against it."

Here our Lord Jesus establishes several key building principles by assuring us of His role and involvement in building His church:

- The church is built on the solid foundation of a revelation of the Person of Christ--*"Upon this rock"*
- He is taking both credit and responsibility for the building process--"*I* will build"
- He assures us that it really will happen, that He is absolutely committed to His Church--"I *will* build"
- He reminds us that it is a process which takes time and requires steps--"I will *build*"
- He is clear with us about ownership, that we are stewards of what really belongs to Him--"*My* church"
- He instills great confidence in our hearts concerning what He builds--*"the gates of hell will not prevail against it"*

Because these promises are so powerful, we could easily miss or dismiss our part. From what Jesus has said, it seems like

He's got it covered! The foundation of the Person and promises of the Lord Jesus Christ found in Matthew 16:18 are so powerful and comprehensive, we could easily wonder if there is anything we can do, really, to build the church.

That's why in 1 Corinthians 3:9-15, God uses the Apostle Paul to write striking and sobering words about the work of building churches that complement so well what Jesus has already said:

> "For we are *God's fellow workers*; *you are* God's field, *God's building*. By the grace God has given me, *I laid a foundation as an expert builder*, and *someone else is building on it*. But each one should be careful how he builds. For no one can lay any foundation other than the one already laid, which is Jesus Christ. If *any man builds* on this foundation using gold, silver, costly stones, wood, hay or straw, his work will be shown for what it is, because the Day will bring it to light. It will be revealed with fire, and the fire will test the quality of each man's work. If what he has built survives, he will receive his reward. If it is burned up, he will suffer loss; he himself will be saved, but only as one escaping through the flames."

Paul's first key insight is that *human involvement is essential* in the building process. We have a vital role in the building process as God's "fellow workers", or co-laborers. We have been given the privilege of working in partnership with Almighty God to build His church! This is an awesome privilege and invitation extended to us. But Paul takes it to another level when he calls himself "an expert builder." The Greek words here are "phronimos", which means thoughtful, wise, and intelligent, and "architekton", from which we derive our word, "architect." It means chief constructor, master builder, or in today's terms, general contractor. While all of us are called to be 'co-laborers' with God, there are some uniquely called and gifted by God as architects, developers, and general contractors in the Spirit to whom God gives wisdom and skill to build. Paul was one of those people. Perhaps you are one, too!

Paul also explains *what* we are building, that we who build churches are *building people*. The Greek word for "building" is oikodome, which means 'an architecturally designed structure where people dwell.' We are building a spiritual structure designed by God called the church, which is made up of people, not a physical building. We are building people who fit together in such a way that they comprise a dwelling place in the Spirit—a corporate structure where God dwells in our midst.

Finally, Paul discusses for us *the materials used* in building. Jesus Christ is always and forever the foundation of every local church and of the global Church. Those who build churches must build in such a way that the foundation is Jesus, through and through. To build on anything else-- personality, hype, good interpersonal skills, marketing, etc.--is not even conceivable to Paul. He simply says, "No other foundation can be laid, because Jesus is already the foundation." He goes on to say that it is possible to have the right foundation and still build with the shoddy materials of wood, hay, and stubble. This ought to be a sober warning to all of us involved in the building process. We are exhorted and invited to build well--with quality materials that will stand the test of fire. I believe that the materials Paul is talking about here--gold, silver, precious stones--are the materials of the kingdom.

Building Kingdom Churches is about how to build churches founded on the Person of Jesus Christ with the principles and practices of the kingdom. Much of what I am writing about is already being lived out by forerunners who embody the kingdom in radical ways as they rapidly advance it throughout the earth. This book has nothing to teach them. Instead, they teach us! Their lives and churches preach. They bring needed conviction to the church in the West.

There are also my mentors here in the West, those who have taught me these principles by example and who have been living them out for many years. They can articulate these things far better than I can, and they are modeling the practice of building kingdom churches in a way that humbles me while stirring holy desire in me to contend for more.

Still, there are many in the Church in the West who are in the throes of change. My deep desire and prayer is that God will use this book to empower a generation of church planters in the West who long for revival and who need handbooks; to help pastors and leadership teams transition from where they are now to where they really want to go; and to give voice to a growing, grassroots swell of believers longing for an expression of church without walls that fits with the priesthood of every believer, a Biblical truth they absolutely know must become an experiential reality in their lifetime.

With the fear of God and great respect for His people, then, I submit this book to the body of Christ in the West. For all those contending for something beyond what we have now, my heart is joined with yours. Let's build what God is building--kingdom churches.

Chapter One
Kingdom REVOLUTION

"...'Once more I will shake...the earth'...The words 'once more' indicate *the removing of what can be shaken...so that what cannot be shaken may remain.* Therefore, since we are receiving a kingdom that cannot be shaken, let us be thankful...for our God is a consuming fire."

--Heb. 12:26-29

Something of great magnitude is impacting the church in the West in our lifetime. We are in the midst of a megashift in paradigm and practice. It is nothing less than a kingdom revolution authored by God that is changing the way we perceive and 'do' church. We are most blessed and least deserving, but God, being rich in mercy, is sending revolution our way.

What a great time to be alive! Should Jesus tarry, historians will surely look back at this time as one where the expression of Christianity in the West shifted dramatically from what we've had to something more radically Biblical, creative, simple, and fiery than anything we've seen in our lifetime. In short, the Lord is releasing understanding and grace to build new kinds of churches. I call them 'kingdom churches' because they contain characteristics combined in such a wonderfully unique way that the kingdom emerges first, ahead of the church, and the King is honored first as Head over every church in a city or region. North America and the West are in desperate need of revolution, and the Lord, in His wisdom and great mercy, in the fullness of time, is releasing a generation to walk in radical kingdom life together, the likes of which we have not seen for some time and perhaps since the early church recorded in the book of Acts.

This is no dramatic overstatement, for surely the Lord's workings are marvelous in our sight. Nor does the grace for this shift constitute bragging rights in any way, since it is largely the combination of the sovereignty of God and the prayers of others gone before us that have brought us to this place. We are entering into the fruit of others' labors, and we are poised in the West to finally make strides to begin to keep pace with our brothers and sisters in such global hot spots as China, Argentina, and various parts of Africa. If you have ever visited these or other places where ongoing revival is taking place, you will recognize the significance of God releasing revolution in the West. It is the kind of truth that might cause us to get on our knees and thank God for His mercy!

> "I revealed myself to those who did not ask for me; I was found by those who did not seek me. To a nation that did not call my name, I said, 'Here am I, here am I.'"
>
> --Isa. 65:1

God is amazingly gracious. He so wants us to 'get' what He is doing that He is going beyond His normal operations (i.e., seek Me to find Me) in order to bring us into a cataclysmic kingdom shift! He has been sovereignly initiating a powerful revolution, and now He is causing us to respond to Him by releasing desire in us for the fullness of what is in His heart! He is truly an amazing God.

Granted, not everyone is able (or willing) to see this shift of epic proportions. But more and more can--and will. The Church in the West has been fast asleep, but she is being awakened by her Lover, the Lord Jesus Christ, and she is responding! Oh, hallelujah! Yes, she is stirring and beginning to rise and take her place beside her King! Love is awakening the church in the West.

This one fact, that the church is getting in touch with how much she is loved by God, is changing everything. Radical change has already begun and is now accelerating! Do you see it?

"Forget the former things; do not dwell on the past. See, I am doing a new thing! Now it springs up; *do you not perceive it?*" --Isa. 43:18-19

Revolution is defined as "*the overthrow of one government and its replacement with another; a sudden or momentous change in a situation.*" The spirit of revolution is shouting loudly from heaven: "The kingdom of the world has become the kingdom of our Lord and of his Christ..." (Rev. 11:15) Could it be true that we are in the midst of a dynamic shift of kingdom revolution?

God is currently helping many people to perceive and to change. In fact, He is raising up a generation with a new default setting for a Christian expression that is deeper, nobler, and stronger than recent generations. My prayer is for the many of us who have been 'asleep' at this hour in the midst of kingdom shaking and shifting. May the Lord be gracious to all of us and reawaken our senses with divine 'smelling salts' to the signs of revolution. They are all around us. Open our eyes, O God!

SIGNS OF REVOLUTION

There are clear, unmistakable evidences that a God-orchestrated revolution is underway. In fact, what God has in mind is so epic that He is using one of His great global strategies to get our attention and to bring about dynamic change in the most rapid way possible. When God wanted to deluge the earth rapidly with a flood of water, He revealed His strategy in Genesis 7:

"...on that day all the *springs of the great deep* burst forth,
and the *floodgates of the heavens* were opened."

--Gen. 7:11

The ground was broken up and the skies were opened up. In the same way, a dynamic shift is bubbling up from within us while God is also downloading it from heaven. There are signs 'from our end', if you will, that represent and point to revolution, while there are also signs 'from His end' that speak to us about His total commitment to change the church in the West. I want to briefly mention four such signs: (1) Holy Dissatisfaction (our end); (2) Global Prayer Movement (our end); (3) Prophetic Declarations (His end); and (4) Cultural Alignment (His end).

Holy Dissatisfaction

Revolution, both natural and spiritual, is always preceded by great dissatisfaction. God releases tremendous groanings and discontent in any people He is desiring to radically touch and change. Dissatisfaction is an essential part of what God is doing. To be successful, revolutionaries need vision for a more desirable future, but they often begin with raw discontent. Vision is defined as "a deep dissatisfaction with what is, coupled with a clear picture of what could be." Before Nehemiah rallied the people to rebuild the wall, he began by weeping over its current state. He gathered the people and began with the bad news. God has been rallying us, and part of His rallying cry has been to place holy dissatisfaction in our hearts and minds that has been growing over the past decade.

This dissatisfaction is not the disgruntled wranglings of a few malcontents. It is a God-orchestrated, holy disquiet meant to produce a deep unwillingness to be satisfied with anything less than the real thing. It is the Lord stirring in His people an unrelenting desire for Himself and His kingdom.

Evidences of holy dissatisfaction have been emerging in the Church for some time now, and they are increasing.

4

What began some years ago as a whisper in the living rooms of a few has become a roar in the mouths of an entire generation unwilling to accept the status quo. People in both the world and the church are standing in solemn protest to the current level and expression of Christianity in much of the church today, especially in the West. This holy protest includes excitement, agitation, and even sadness.

Within the ranks of American Christianity in particular there is a growing sense of discontent and discontinuity. I see it in general among both pastors and people in the church. Many of those in "full-time ministry" that I know personally or hear from in some other way are expressing a deep, heart-felt desire to see "the way we do church" radically change. Full-time paid pastors are leaving their posts at local churches in record numbers. While they began in ministry with a confidence that they could make a difference, many are finding the slow, cumbersome process of change in church life too difficult to bear. They are, understandably, 'opting out.' Whether this migration is from the Lord, the enemy, or both, it is nonetheless an indicator of holy discontent and of a church system in radical need of change.

The people, too, who occupy the pews of churches across the nation have for years been faithfully attending while a great burden, even a sadness, grows in their hearts. They may not know exactly why they feel what they feel, but they know instinctively that the church, while made up of people they love very much, is largely ineffective. Some of these ones are also 'opting out' in silent protest, and they are not 'snapping out of it' as some would like. They refuse shallow comforts and appeals.

> "When I was in distress, I sought the LORD; at night I stretched out untiring hands and my soul refused to be comforted. I remembered you, O God, and I groaned; I mused, and my spirit grew faint. Selah." --Ps. 77:2-3

Even among the better churches in the West, there is often a delightfully painful phenomenon happening. On the one

5

hand, there is tremendous gratitude for all God is currently doing--from someone's marriage being saved, to a body being healed, to a needy family befriended and helped. It's good fruit, it's what we all signed up for, and we're glad every time it happens. Yet, with all the great things that are happening, the pain and restlessness in the hearts of many remains. There is a groaning for more! While this groaning can never be fully satisfied this side of heaven, I do believe that God has much more for His church (and therefore for the world) before the return of His Son. 1 Cor. 2:9 assures us that "eye has not seen and ear has not heard all that God has prepared for those who love Him." While some of this is reserved for heaven, some is for now, and we can press the future into the present through believing prayer. God has reserved much in this hour for those who will apprehend it by faith. This is the posture of those who will see a kingdom revolution in their lifetime. It is a groaning that cannot (and must not) be suppressed, because it is fueled by ardent desire and longing for the real thing.

Over the years I have listened to many, among both church leaders and members, who have expressed this groaning. I can hear conversations in my brain, words echoing, words couched in reverence for God and love for the church, but words nonetheless that speak of a deeper longing, a dissatisfaction. They are summed up in this: "While I am thankful for what we have, we're not even close to where we're meant to be." That doesn't diminish our progress--it only highlights our need. We are hungry for more.

Global Prayer Movement

Thankfully, this holy disquiet has given birth to an intercessory groaning that is now forming into the greatest prayer movement in the history of the church. While the people of God have always prayed throughout history, it is a clear sign of change when the church, particularly in the

West, begins to fervently and consistently cry out like never before.

"My house will be called a house of prayer for all the peoples." --Isa. 56:7

Of course, this verse means so much more than simply renaming your church. It is God Himself giving definition and substance to the church in the future. There will come a day, God says, when prayers both from My people and from those trying to find me will define the nature and activity of my house to such an extent that the only appropriate way to think of and speak about the church will be to characterize it as a 'house of prayer.' The activity of prayer in His house includes both intercession from His people and prayers of salvation from the lost, as God creates an inextricable link between the activity of prayer and the evangelism of the nations.

Jesus was so intense about this reality that when he witnessed what had up to then been considered a little harmless profiteering going on in the temple courts, He became more fiery and indignant than perhaps any other time in his ministry. The activity of prayer in His house was so essential, and the invitation for the lost to come to the court of the gentiles to pray was so paramount, that He was zealous to remove anything that hindered this primary preoccupation:

"Jesus went straight to the Temple and threw out everyone who had set up shop, buying and selling. He kicked over the tables of loan sharks and the stalls of dove merchants. He quoted this text: 'My house was designated a house of prayer; You have made it a hangout for thieves.'"
--Mt. 21:12-13, *The Message*

Notice that God's people have been designated, marked, and branded as destined for prayer. As prayer is becoming more widespread, there are literal houses of prayer springing up

7

across the land in North America and all over the world. Throughout America's heartland, for example, there are actual places of night and day prayer that have been going on for over several years with hundreds involved. This team of forerunners is modeling for and imparting to the nations the practice of unceasing prayer until the return of Jesus. This is right! The prayer movement is springing forth from the inward places of the church as a clear sign of revolution.

Prophetic Declarations

Revolution often begins with a revolt against the current established culture of thought process and structure. The need for change is always seen first by those with prophetic insight and keen revelation. Simple prophecy in the New Testament church consists of "edification, exhortation, and comfort" for the building up of the saints (1 Cor. 14:3), something we are to desire earnestly (1 Cor. 14:1). But there are other, valid dimensions and purposes of the New Testament prophetic gift, such as when Agabus warned Paul of things to come (Acts 21:10-12). I believe the church needs men and women who 'watch' and pray, who see what is happening, both good and bad, and who alert the church so she can take appropriate action. Sometimes the appropriate action is repentance.

Prophetic people have been chafing against the status quo (as God intends for them to do) for some years now, and as a result, they have sometimes been labeled as 'negative' and even 'rebellious.' In some cases, there is indeed negativity and sometimes rebellion. However, the key issue here is that they have been seeing and hearing correctly. There is indeed something to prophesy *against!* The way we've been 'doing church' in America and in the West, with the exception of a few notably excellent churches here and there, has been largely ineffective and, at times, even unbiblical. And God Himself is objecting through His people.

God is speaking *through* His people *to* His people about these epic shifts. There is a multitude of prophetic voices, and not just among charismatics, who are saying the same thing. In fact, there are so many prophets and prophetic people saying the same thing that within the scope of this book, all I can do is summarize. If you are in touch with what prophetic people have been saying lately, you know that the message over recent years has consistently been: *The church is going to radically change.* The nature and expression of Christianity will change rapidly. God Himself is declaring it prophetically! *And it's already happening.*

George Barna, perhaps America's premiere church statistician and researcher and I believe a prophetic voice to the church, has written several books that serve as the warnings of a faithful watchman. In one of his more recent books entitled, <u>The Second Coming Of The Church</u>. He writes these sobering words:

> "Let's cut to the chase. After nearly two decades of studying Christian churches in America, I'm convinced that the typical church as we know it today has a rapidly expiring shelf life...Today's church is incapable of responding to the present moral crisis. It must reinvent itself or face virtual oblivion by mid-21st century.

> "A serious condition calls for a serious remedy. The time for study commissions and ecumenical debates is past. Merely tinkering with processes and structures will not do. Praying for better times is a necessary but insufficient tonic. Where a dose of strong medicine may have healed some of our infirmities in the past, we now require major reconstructive surgery if we are to move beyond reliance upon self-support systems. Our goal cannot simply be a timid, powerless survival. It must be the role that Christ called the Church to play, that of a loving, authoritative, healing, and compelling influence on the world...We desperately need a holistic revolution of mind, heart, and spirit."

Yes, God is speaking through the prophets in our day about a cataclysmic shift, and a growing symphony of voices is rising as incense before Him and as a trumpet to His people. The prophet Joel spoke to the people of his day much the same way God is alerting the church today in Joel 2:15-17--

> "Blow a trumpet in Zion, consecrate a fast, proclaim a solemn assembly, gather the people, sanctify the congregation, assemble the elders, gather the children and the nursing infants. Let the bridegroom come out of his room and the bride out of her bridal chamber. Let the priests, the LORD's ministers, weep between the porch and the altar, and let them say, 'Spare Your people, O LORD, and do not make Your inheritance a reproach, a byword among the nations. Why should they among the peoples say, 'Where is their God?'"

I love the church, because the church is the Bride of Christ, and His Bride deserves honor and respect. It is no denigration of that Bride, however, to see that she has some "spots and wrinkles" on her gown. Without acknowledging these, we will not be able to "make ourselves ready" for the wedding feast of the Lamb. There are real reasons for holy dissatisfaction among the prophetic voices to our generation! God has a right to voice His objections to the state of the church in the West. Honestly, the landscape of the church is littered with attitudes, mindsets, spirits, and problems we have brought in from the world. In part, we have made the church into something that God never intended. The list is long, but here are four examples of the kinds of things He is objecting to through prophetic voices:

Consumerism. The spirit of consumerism is so pervasive that we can hardly detect it, because it feels right. It is characterized by "You can (and should) make me happy, so pray for me, meet my needs, get me motivated, make me feel special and included. If you don't, I will go someplace else where they can do these things for me." Of course, for a Christian to actually voice these words would sound so unspiritual. Yet this is often how we really think. Consumerism has bred in us an entitlement mentality. Many in our churches are struggling because of consumerism. It is driving them from place to place, and they are not finding the rest Christ offers. The cultural shift from responsibility to rights that typifies our society today has also permeated the atmosphere of the church. Too many of us view the church much like the old 70s show, "The Love Boat." You know, the show where every person is pampered by a large, well-trained staff looking after every need. The church was never designed to be "The Love Boat" (although it was designed to be a vessel full of love!). It was always meant to be more like a fishing boat, with everyone working, everyone helping to catch and clean the fish, and everyone coming away at the end of the day knowing that they gave their all to gather in the largest and best possible haul of fish.

Introspection. I believe in recovery, inner healing, and so on. And I'm grateful not only for the healing God has done in my own life, but also for that which he continues to do in the church. I appreciate and admire those who provide ongoing therapy for parts of the church who are deeply hurting. Yet, the therapy culture in the church has birthed a mind set that says, "I can't serve the Lord until I feel better." While this is true in some cases of extreme wounding, the problem is that too few among us actually learn how to function in the midst of our pain. Instead, people quit serving God because our hurts are bigger than God's call to lay down our lives. A culture of therapy stands in opposition to being a missional, outward-focused people who lay down our lives for the many lost people Jesus came to seek and save. There is balance in everything, but waiting until we're completely whole before we obey Him is not God's heart. We lose our lives in order to gain them.

Introspection can lead to a spirit of poverty, where the unspoken idea is: "If I really expend myself with the little bit I do have, then I won't have anything left...so I'll protect instead of share." This affects our attitude toward money, time, and general output. We are fearful of committing to various ministries because of what will be required of us. When we live in fear of the free time we might not get, or the things our children might not get, we deny ourselves what we were created for--to love God and people in practical ways by serving and laying down our lives. Jesus stands in opposition to this mentality when He says, "For the Son of man did not come to be served, but to serve, and to give His life as a ransom for many." Freely we have received, and to break a spirit of poverty, we must freely give from the place of a life wholly given to God.

Individualism. Individualism can originate from pride ("Don't tell me what to do", and "I can do it myself") or fear ("If I let someone else in, I could get hurt" and "What if they take my place or somehow devalue me?"). Whatever its source, individualism focuses almost exclusively on the individual aspects of Christianity--praying, reading our Bibles, listening to Christian music--while largely missing the fact that Christianity is always and forever centered in a community of faith. The New Testament "you" is like the Spanish "ustedes" or the Southern "y'all." Paul's letters are written mostly to churches and mostly in the plural form. Even the seemingly right emphasis in recent years on gift evaluation has inadvertently helped people to focus on their own gift, often producing picky servants who only do what their gift indicates. This seems right until you compare the church to a family (which it is), where everyone has to do chores that may not necessarily fall within their gifting. The heart of the Biblical church in the New

Testament had to do with servanthood, preferring, and the commonality they shared.

Spectatorism. Many church historians trace this problem back to about 312 A.D., the era in which Constantine endorsed Christianity as favored religion. With that declaration began the great Christian building campaign, and it has never really stopped--at least in the West. Christian churches and cathedrals sprang up throughout the land. Eventually a professional clergy developed, where certain people were paid to perform church functions and duties for everyone else. With Christians no longer persecuted, a sense of cultural ease set in. *Church became something that you did rather than who you are.* Ministry became something professionals did for the rest of the Christians, rather than the church being a living body, a priesthood of all believers. Spectator Christianity involves compartmentalization, segmenting our lives into sound bites and blocks of time in our busy schedule. Church can easily become one of our time-slot-fillers. The early church met daily from house to house and in the temple courts. No one was needy, because people laid down their lives for one another in radical ways. Some would even sell their house and give the money just to make sure everyone was taken care of. Church in the West, unfortunately, is often not about a radical army of people connected through vital relationships; instead, it is often still considered a building we meet in and a staff that we pay. The inevitable result is that we are religious spectators. Jesus continues to challenge our idea of what a disciple is. He lays down the requirements plainly by calling us to daily denial, discipline, and devotion (Lk. 9:23). Forget milk--Got courage? Discipleship is radical, full-time participation with Him.

Cultural Alignment

It is a surprising, intriguing, and disheartening reality that sometimes secular Western culture is more responsive to the leading of the Holy Spirit than the church. Secular people with God-given prophetic gifting see the future with great clarity, even though their revelation is incomplete and often tainted. And how do they respond to the revelation God gives them? They immediately trumpet that revelation through the media of movies, books, newspaper and magazine articles, songs, and dramatic arts.

Meanwhile, and often many months or even years later, little clusters of church people are having discussions about the symbolic significance of such movies as *Field Of Dreams* and *The Matrix*. Those in churches who see analogies in movies are sometimes labeled as 'secular' and 'worldly', but such labeling completely misses the point. God intends to reveal parables to the culture only *after* He has already spoken to the church. The church is meant to lead the world in hearing God's voice and shaping culture. But the church in the West has had so much difficulty receiving and obeying a fresh word from God that He often uses a secondary, less desirable method of communication, such as a 'secular' movie. He knows where He can find His people far too often--sitting in movie theaters or at home in front of their televisions! So He hopes they will listen there.

> "For God speaks in one way, yet in another, though men
> may not perceive it." --Job 33:14

Years ago, Kevin Prosch wrote a song called, "God Is Speaking Through The Music." Stated more broadly, God is speaking through the culture. For example, take the frequent discussion of our "postmodern" culture (or don't!). The issue of how the church is interacting with what is now commonly called "postmodernity" is an example of our tardiness and defensive posture. So many books on postmodernity have made their way onto the shelves of nearly every pastor and church in America that I am reticent to even broach the subject. With all the great insights into the culture, we are still often missing the core issue. God is not asking the church to clue in to postmodern culture so it can catch up or keep in step with it. The idea that we must carefully examine the culture to figure out how to adjust church in order to make people's church experience more palatable is a shallow, church-growth oriented bandaid to a much deeper issue.

God is speaking *through* the culture! And He is telling us, I believe rather plainly, that the culture is positioned for revival. God Himself has shaped the culture of the Western world to prepare it to receive the gospel. Instead of haranguing the church about its need to understand the culture, we need the more relevant, fresher Godward message that the culture is strategically positioned by a sovereign God to see the 'sleeping giant' called the church wake up, stand up, and walk in radical Christianity. They're ready for us to become who we were always meant to be. Could it be that God is using the culture to unlock passionate Christianity in the church? It's happening. The culture is calling us!

Because God is speaking through the culture, He is not stressed out or wringing His hands! He is speaking, rather loudly I might add, to His church. Through the culture, God is communicating many things to His people, most of which we don't have space to elaborate on within the scope of this book. I want to briefly review three examples of what I believe God is saying through the culture: (1) Acceleration; (2) Participation; and (3) Reality.

Acceleration. Individuals, families, and businesses are juggling more issues and processing more information than ever before. Things are speeding up! Acceleration is not an unhealthy attachment to adrenaline or to the Protestant work ethic. It has to do with an explosion of creative change in our culture that preaches to the church. Culture in the West is rapidly reinventing itself, perhaps as frequently as every two years. The rapid advances in technology allow for change to occur more often and more suddenly. And, because it is cultural, it is becoming the norm. In this, God is speaking to the church. The culture is begging the church to accept change as normal and therefore to become more creative, more spontaneous, and frankly more Biblical in its thinking. This acceleration of change has nothing to do with the changeless aspects of the Christian faith, like the timeless message of the gospel. Nor is it necessarily to be interpreted as a need to have cooler video presentations and more graphically interesting bulletins and web sites (i.e., to be more 'hip'). It has to do with a revival-based thought process, where it no longer takes twenty years to produce a nominal Christian! It is embracing what Rolland Allen calls "the spontaneous expansion of the church." Acceleration is about a profound belief in the raw power of God to produce what our program-based design churches have had difficulty producing.

> "If you have run with footmen and they have tired you out, then how can you compete with horses? If you fall down in a land of peace, how will you do in the thicket of the Jordan?"   --Jer. 12:5

Acceleration is about streamlining. Time being what it is, and busyness being what it is, the culture of today cannot and will not waste its time supporting traditions of the past. For a person today to be involved in anything, it must be truly significant and impacting. This is a clear invitation to the church to jettison sacred cows and abandon unnecessary, redundant meetings so our efforts can be more simple, streamlined, and focused. How refreshing! The culture is calling for the church to obey the Scriptural command to "make the most of every opportunity" (cf. Eph. 5:16; Col. 4:5) and to return to the "simplicity and purity of devotion to Christ" (2 Cor. 11:3).

We also streamline to learn to move at a different pace than we have in the past. God is using the culture to preach toward a change in the default setting of our pace as a Christian people. The Bible refers to several different postures before God, some of which speak of momentum and pace. We are called to lie down (Ps. 23:2), to kneel (Ps. 95:6), to sit (Eph. 2:6), to stand (Eph. 6:13-14), to walk (Gal. 5:16), and to run (Heb. 12:1). The church in the West is learning to stand in our authority in Christ against the enemy, for example, but we have not yet learned to really 'run' together as we advance God's kingdom together. Wherever revival is occurring in our day, they have learned how to run together. God is taking the church in the West to a place where we can run together. Acceleration is Biblical and prophetically timely. It is a paradigm shift that the culture is preaching to the church.

Participation. We live in a culture of participation that wants to be involved in the experiences of real life. People base more and more of their decisions on inductive, experiential reasoning than deductive, 'right' answers. The church has been stressing over this, decrying the departure from absolute truth. But this is not stressworthy. This cultural shift is a huge advantage for the church that can provide real encounters with God. Modernity replaced heart-felt faith with mere intellectual folly by exalting human technocracy. After centuries of seeing that rational, detached modernity cannot and will not answer the deepest issues of humanity, our current postmodern world is reaching out for supernatural experiences. While it is entirely appropriate for the church to avoid certain demonic movies and television shows, we must stop seeing this expression of the supernatural as anything other than a move of God on the culture. People want to encounter God! They want to see heaven! They want to see the beautiful Son of Man with hair white like wool, with eyes like flames of fire, with a face ten thousand times brighter than the sun!

To make matters better, this participatory cultural megashift means that people don't want to experience God alone. The rugged individualism that has characterized America is rapidly changing. The modern man was "a rock" and "an island." The postmodern person is looking for real significance in relationship and community. This isn't just an insecure need to belong. There is a strong desire to be a part of real community and to walk through spiritual experiences with those who can mentor them in the things of God. God is calling the church to step up to the plate and be those mentors. This challenges our own participation and experience in the things of God. The messenger truly is the message. We help people encounter God because we are encountering God. This is the kind of participation needed in kingdom churches--those who are experiencing what they're telling others about.

Reality. "What worked for our parents doesn't necessarily work for us" is not just a generational mantra; it is a cultural megashift. People are throwing overboard anything that bogs down their sense of reality and their search for meaning. Truth is valued, but moralism has little value in today's culture. People today are looking for truth, and they're willing to look anywhere, especially in the supernatural, to find something real. People approach life mosaically, like a quilter--a bit of fabric from this religion, another bit of fabric from that experience, to make life's quilt. Guess what? That makes them more open to the power of God flowing in and through the church. This is a good thing! It's time to stop apologizing for a gospel filled with power and to start welcoming the invasion of the supernatural into our developed world.

This culture, along with this generation, has been the single-most overstimulated culture in existence to date. Information is being transferred and assimilated at such an incredibly rapid rate that very little if anything surprises, shocks, or entertains. This is a culture where "what you see is what you get" is the norm. The good news for the church is that we don't have to entertain (nor were we ever meant to!). We can go straight for the heart, because God has made our culture ready! We do not have to beat around the bush. Our culture is deeply desiring the undiluted reality of a God who loves them passionately. If the culture ever needed a straight dose of Jesus Christ, full strength, without any additives (or subtractions), it is right now. Demons are having free reign on our televisions, in our movies, and in the minds of our young people, and the people in our culture need more than intriguing 'conversation.' Do we have the power of Elijah to challenge the prophets of Baal? This is the church's moment of truth and, I believe, her finest hour! People in our culture need to be delivered by someone with some anointing from God and the guts to call it like it is. Sensitivity, thoughtfulness, and tact, yes, good social skills, OK, but beyond that, let's help a generation to encounter the same living God that the prophets of Baal had to deal with. Our God is truly a consuming fire.

These cultural megashifts are highly significant for the church. It is as if a road has been paved into the realm of revolution. God has caused the culture to pave the way for the church! This is not a time for the church to reproduce our familiar forms geared toward predictability and tameness. No! Many people in and out of our churches are not encountering God in a real way--but they long to. This cultural megashift has large implications on how we think about and "do" church.

We need to be interested in cultural megashifts at this time because people in the West are moving from a purely Western rationale mind set to more of an Eastern (and culturally Biblical) way of thinking. And the church has an amazing opportunity to jettison worldly practices, reinvent itself and "go Biblical" on the culture! Cultural megashifts are like flashing neon lights inviting the church into a kingdom revolution. "Here we are!" the culture is saying. "Come and get us!" May the Lord give us understanding.

DIVINE DISMANTLING

Have you ever had the experience of barbecuing while everyone is standing around, waiting for the meat to 'get done'? Before God can serve up the revolution we are hungry for, He has to make sure we're 'done.' I believe that the church in the West is about done! Better stated, we're finally getting 'undone.' These are the ways of God as He shared them with His prophet Jeremiah:

> "See, today I appoint you over nations and kingdoms to *uproot* and *tear down*, to *destroy* and *overthrow*, to *build* and to *plant.*" --Jer. 1:10

God has been bringing about the right conditions for revolution. He has birthed within the church a holy dissatisfaction that has led to a global prayer movement. Prophetic voices have been trumpeting the need for change, while the culture has been aligning itself to the purposes of God. And the net result is that the church in the West is becoming a people who are 'undone.' There has been a divine dismantling of the ship called the church in the West, and the Lord has been doing the dismantling.

If you have felt hungry, weak, longing, confused and yet somehow hopeful, you are not alone. Millions of Christians are going through a paradigm shift in this very hour, and God is orchestrating it! He is preparing His people and the culture for radical change, and I believe we are going to see both darkness getting darker and the light of God through His people becoming brighter and brighter. This will be the church's finest hour.

DOORWAY TO REVOLUTION

God never wastes a sign. He puts them there for a reason. The signs of revolution indicate a destination. We are going somewhere! The rest of this book is an attempt to give voice and bring some level of clarity to the whys and hows of kingdom revolution that will lead us to build kingdom churches well. I want to finish this chapter with a couple of thoughts about what kind of heart posture is needed to begin to enter into the process of building kingdom churches.

It's About Faith

Perceiving what God is doing is not automatic. Many in the Western church have adopted a "been there, done that, bought the t-shirt" attitude when it comes to radical change in the church. "Can any good thing come out of the Western church?" they ask. The Scriptures clearly warn us not to develop a cynical attitude towards the prophetic message God is sending to His people:

> "Do not put out the Spirit's fire; do not treat prophecies with contempt." --1 Thess. 5:19-20

This was the mistake made by the strong, self-assured military officer that served as an assistant to the king of Israel in the time of Elisha the prophet. During a time of severe famine, Elisha prophesied that suddenly, in one day, the famine would not only be over, but food would be so amazingly abundant that its price would be very inexpensive (2 Kings

7:1). This required such a phenomenal miracle that the officer said to Elisha, "Look, even if the LORD should open the floodgates of the heavens, how could this happen?" Even though it seemed far-fetched, the officer didn't properly esteem what God was saying. The results were tragic:

> "You will see it with your own eyes," answered Elisha, "but you will not eat any of it!" --2 Kings 7:2

God understands our propensity towards unbelief, especially when it comes to dead things coming alive, or dry things being drenched, or scattered things coming together. For Him, it is not a problem, but for us, we can hardly conceive of it. God came to one of His most faithful prophets, Ezekiel, who was privileged with great revelation, and He showed Ezekiel a large valley full of dry bones, after which God asked him a question: "Son of man, can these bones live?" Today, God is asking us a similar question: "Church, do you believe that I can bring revolution in your generation?"

Over the doorway of this revolution is the word 'faith.' The Bible says that without faith, it is impossible to please God, and yet, Jesus throws us a curve ball when He asks the question: "When the Son of Man returns, will He find faith on the earth?" (Lk. 18:8)

Faith is needed in transition, and the church is in transition. This transition is vital, but it is also painful. Just at the end of pregnancy and just before the joy of birth is "transition." Transition is when you have watched and waited for so long to see the church come into a place of maturity and fullness, and then when it starts to happen, you experience even more pain. Transition is when your hope has been deferred so that you have become heart sick, and when you hear vision announced and prophesied, your mind knows that you agree but your heart is unable to feel excitement. Transition is when you have paid a great price in the secret womb of intercession to see something birthed, only to have strange people yelling "Push!" in your face!

Every time I have been waterskiing, faith has been required, because there is a place between when you say "Hit it!" to when you're standing up and enjoying skiing that the water is spraying in your face and you can't see, and you have to remember what works--which is counterintuitive. This is especially true with 'slow' water ski boats! The longer it takes for the boat to pull you up, the harder it is to stand up. Faith is required to water ski, to deliver a baby, and to move from where we've been to where we're going as the church. And the boat has been slow! But God is in the business of filling us afresh with new faith for the journey we are on. Have faith in God! He will surely have His way on the earth. The church will be unified, and the church will be one in heart and mind, because Jesus' prayers are always answered, and He prayed for unity! The church will not always be about the glory of man, because "the Lord alone will be exalted in that day." The church will experience the glory of God, because "the glory of the latter house will be greater than the former", and because God has promised through Habakkuk that "the glory of the Lord will cover the earth as the waters cover the sea!" The dream in your heart for His church will happen. It was given by God, and He intends to see it come to pass. Rest in His ability.

It's About A Recipe

One of the most common and compelling questions for those of us on the journey of discovery into a new kind of church is, "So, what's it going to look like?" This is a fair question. Revelation is progressive, and because it always begins with prophetic groanings, we've mostly had dissatisfaction and questions. We have spent a solid decade 'deconstructing' and critiquing Western Christianity. It really is time for some answers!

Once, when I was praying about this issue, I sensed the Lord speak to my heart, "Mark, it's about a recipe." I understood Him to mean that all of the ingredients for a kingdom church are already in the earth, but a recipe combines these ingredients in new amounts and in a new way so as to create a brand new dish that tastes delicious to those partaking of its outcome.

A recipe is defined as "a set of directions with a list of ingredients for making or preparing something" and "a means to a desired end." I believe God is releasing understanding and strategy for new kinds of churches: kingdom churches. These churches will look mostly familiar to the casual observer, because there will be familiar ingredients of prayer, gatherings, leadership, outreach, worship, and so on. But the underlying "cooking" philosophy, the amount of the ingredients, how they're combined, and what is done with them will surely be different. Each kingdom church will be unique in its recipe, but "the set of directions with a list of ingredients" is vital. This book is an attempt to articulate some of these ingredients and how to apportion them in a fresh way.

Function Over Form

In order for something new to live, something old needs to give. As God is changing the church, we cannot remain smug and comfortable and also be filled with the adventure of the journey. We cannot cling to the railings of our pews so tightly and also have revolution. Something is going to have to go for new life to come. My vote is that we lay down our preconceived notions of church life and allow the Holy Spirit to come and breathe fresh wind in our sails. May the Lord raise up kingdom churches throughout the land as a generation of revivalists take their place. Let's embrace kingdom revolution!

Chapter Two
Kingdom MOTIVATION

"But seek *first* the kingdom of God and His righteousness,
and all these things will be given to you as well."

--Matt. 6:33

I remember a particular leadership meeting about 15 years
ago as though it were yesterday. A pastor of a rapidly
growing church (and therefore an 'expert' on why and how
churches grow) was speaking to the leadership of our church
on principles of church growth. His talk was interesting and
compelling, not unlike other talks I had heard on this subject.
As I listened to him speak about assimilation plans, sanctuary
layout, worship/congregation dynamics, people flow, being
culturally relevant, and so on, my mind drifted back to when I
was a teenager...

Shortly after becoming a Christian at 16 years old, I
began reading missionary biographies of people like Jim
Elliot, Hudson Taylor, and David Brainerd, along with many
books on prayer, with the stories of intercessors like Rees
Howells and John 'Praying' Hyde touching my heart and
forming my thinking. How I wanted to go to the mission field
at that time! My burning desire was to take the gospel to the
poor. I wanted to see for myself that the gospel would work
without the 'props' of the Western world...

Back to the meeting. As I listened to this man speak, I
knew him to be a great guy who wanted good things for the
church in general as well as for the denomination we were
part of. At that time in my life, I was just stepping into paid
ministry, and I didn't know very much about anything! He

25

was clearly the expert, and I was definitely one of the greenhorns sitting in the meeting. Nevertheless, as he talked further, somehow I knew that he and I were not on the same page. In my gut, I felt that some of the core motivations of the church growth movement that he was espousing were missing the point. I knew that there was something more raw and more real God was after, but I couldn't articulate what I was feeling. So I raised my hand and asked him a sincere question: "Why can't we do church on dirt floors like they do in Africa? Why do we really need all this stuff? I mean, if God shows up, and if people are getting saved and healed, what difference does it make?" The intention of my question was not to devalue thoughtful planning, but rather to get at the heart and essence of what the church is. He smiled, tilted his head just a little, and replied, "You do it [church] your way, and I'll do it my way, and let's see who impacts more people." I didn't ask any more questions that day! His answer, though, only strengthened my growing conviction that the motivation of much of the church in the West had drifted from what God originally intended for His people.

It's funny how things come full circle. Not too long ago I found myself in Mozambique, Africa, amidst a modern-day revival. Blind eyes are opening, the dead are being raised, the poor are being fed, the gospel is being preached, the church is being equipped and sent out, and people are coming to Christ in droves every week. In fact, speaking of church growth and multiplication, when I was there they were planting about 30 churches every week, and they had seen several thousand churches planted in less than a decade, all from new converts. They were living my teenage dream! I remember being in the midst of several dozen Mozambican pastors with my face in the dirt, sobbing uncontrollably, humbled in their presence and hungering after God with them.

Not too many months later, I was home in California with our church on a Sunday morning, and we were having a celebration in the school gymnasium we rent. It was a powerful time, and at the end, I gave an altar call. Most of the people came up front, responding to the Spirit of God. The fear of the Lord was evident in that meeting, and we were on our faces on the gym floor. But this wasn't just any gym floor. A few months before, there had been a flood, and the wood floor had been removed, leaving only concrete and old glue. Because the new wood floor had not yet been installed, the school itself was neither using nor cleaning the gym, and a significant layer of dirt had accumulated on the floor. So here we were, on our knees and faces before God, on the dirt-laden concrete floor in the Central Coast of California, and it reminded me, ever so slightly, of some of my experiences in Africa. I sensed the pleasure of the Lord as He watched His people humbling themselves and hungering after Him, and I was grateful to see so many otherwise well-groomed, 'cool' California people going after God with abandon, even on a 'dirt' floor! Then I remembered the leadership meeting 15 years ago, and I smiled.

God looks at things differently than we do. A recurring rebuke in the Scriptures is captured in Psalm 50:21, where the Lord says, "These things you have done and I kept silent; *you thought I was altogether like you.* But I will rebuke you..." Isaiah 55 tells us that the ways of God are higher than our ways and His thoughts are higher than ours, in *every way.* These verses (and others like them) indicate that we need to check our motivation, because God sees from a superior vantage point, and we are prone to look at things differently than God. Perhaps this concept is best illustrated when Samuel, God's prophet, went to the house of Jesse on assignment from God to anoint the next king of Israel. In the midst of examining each of the various brothers to see whom God has selected, Samuel eyed Eliab and thought that surely this was the guy! Evidently Eliab had impressive outward, physical qualities, perhaps even a certain 'air' of dignity, that compelled Samuel to hastily conclude that he was the Lord's choice. But God catches the motivation of Samuel's heart, and in that moment speaks a powerful word to him and to us:

"Do not consider his appearance or his height, for I have rejected him. The LORD *does not look at the things man looks at.* Man looks at the outward appearance, but the LORD looks at the heart." --1 Sam. 16:7

If the LORD does not look at the things men look at, then to be 'successful' at building His kind of churches (kingdom churches), we need to lay hold of the things that motivate and attract God, not us. We need to look where He's looking. So where is God looking?

WHOLEHEARTED LOVERS

"The eyes of the Lord look to and fro throughout the earth, that He might strongly support the one whose heart is completely His." --2 Chron. 16:9

By far the most profound change occurring in the church today is the growing preoccupation of the church with the Person of God. The church is falling in love! The world will grow in amazement while the devil experiences more and more consternation that the first commandment is taking first place in the hearts and minds of God's people. While this has been true in geographic pockets and historical periods, never has there been such a widespread, growing obsession to give ourselves in extravagant devotion to Jesus Christ. The core motivation of the church is beginning to align with the Father's original intention to focus on His Son.

I once heard someone say, "People who are in love outperform people who are not in love two to one." This is true! I remember as a young man in my twenties courting the young woman who is now my wife. Staying up late, getting up early, doing extra favors, these were 'effortless' compared to just a few months earlier before I knew her. I was falling in love, and I was 'outperforming' my previous self! At the end of 1 Corinthians 12, Paul said that the way of love is "a more excellent way." God is hand-picking people to build kingdom churches. His eyes are searching the earth for wholehearted lovers. They march to the beat of a different drummer. They are unmoved and unmotivated by many of the things that motivated the church in the latter part of the 20th century, like church size, prestige in the community, and so on. They are motivated by love.

> "For the love of Christ motivates us." --2 Cor. 5:14

This statement by the Apostle Paul had everything to do with an all-out approach to winning lost people fueled by a heart of love. In 1 Cor. 9:22, Paul said it this way: "I have become all things to all men so that by all possible means I might save some." Paul was essentially saying, "Love burns inside me, and I will do pretty much anything to win lost people to my Friend and King, Jesus." For the apostle, form followed function. It wasn't about "church growth." It was about a burning passion of love to win people to Jesus!

Laid Down Lovers

This issue of love has profound impact on how we do church. Recently, someone I deeply respect, a proven lover of God and a global leader in the church, was sitting with me in a strategy meeting. In the midst of it, she turned to me and said, "I don't mind if people make strategies as long as they are on their faces doing it." She was referring to the fact that we have no business doing the King's business if we're not preoccupied with the King rather than His business! We are called to be a people in love, undone by His beauty, laid down, on our faces in His presence, falling deeper in love, completely childlike and dependent.

I do not believe it is wrong to seek God's hand of blessing. In fact, we need God's hand of blessing, and we are encouraged to ask God to bless us and to provide for us. The popular prayer of Jabez is a noteworthy example. But as people who are desiring churches that are different than what we have been producing, we must, in real practice, put God first, not merely as a theological priority, but as a heart-pounding reality. Only when our primary obsession is His Person can we begin to have the right perspective and motivation to carry out the things He desires for us to do.

David said in the familiar Psalm 27:4, "One thing I have desired from the LORD, and that will I seek: to behold the beauty of the LORD, and to meditate in His temple." When the Apostle Paul was knocked off his horse, he asked two questions that hold significance for us: "Who are you, Lord?" and "What do you want me to do?" When we ask these two God-ward questions, in their proper order, on a continual basis, as a people in love, then we can build kingdom churches well. Loving God in practice is a prerequisite to building kingdom churches.

Love purifies our motivation by removing false, lesser motives in us and by giving us the energy to lay down our lives just because of love. God so loved the world that He gave. The deeper the love, the more the sacrifice. A people in love are dangerous to the camp of the enemy, because they don't care anymore. They don't care about fame, they're not after titles, they don't really notice whether or not they have more people in their Sunday meeting than the church down the street. Such thoughts don't even register on the radar screen of their hearts. The enemy is deeply afraid of the Bride falling in love with her Bridegroom. Like David in Psalm 27, she would be fearless:

> "The LORD is my light and my salvation--whom shall I fear? The LORD is the stronghold of my life--of whom shall I be afraid? Though an army besiege me, my heart will not fear; though war break out against me, even then I will be confident." --Ps. 27:1, 3

Yes, there is a very, very dangerous generation arising! The forces of hell are trembling. This generation will build different kinds of churches, churches that are free from a political spirit, churches that truly rejoice to see others succeed, churches that are in love with their community and bored with small-mindedness and lesser motivations. Kingdom churches are filled with people in love, laid-down lovers living life out of God's heart.

KINGDOM FIRST

The natural byproduct of a people in love is that they seek to walk in and advance God's kingdom ahead of everything else. When the eyes of the Lord find people who are wholehearted lovers of God, He finds a people of His kingdom. This "kingdom first" perspective affects everything having to do with church. In order to understand the power of "kingdom first" as it relates to doing church, we must first have a solid grasp of the centrality and significance of the kingdom.

Defining The Kingdom Of God

To put it simply, kingdom is **rule**. The Greek word is *basileia*, which refers to the realm or base of power by which a king rules. There are two aspects to kingdom. The first is the *right* to rule. In ancient and current societies with a government of monarchy, those kings or queens have a right to rule their realm, which includes all of the physical territory and the content of that territory, including people and possessions. In that sense, God's kingdom is the entire universe, and, as it concerns us, the earth. Psalm 115:3 declares, "Our God is in the heavens, He does whatever He pleases." That is the sovereignty of the King of the universe. Our God has the right to rule anywhere He wishes, because it all belongs to Him. In that sense, his kingdom is everywhere.

However, there is a second, more immediate aspect to this business of kingdom. Kingdom refers not only to God's right to rule, but also to *the actual places where God rules*. In other words, wherever God is indeed ruling, there is the kingdom. Where is the will of the king being expressed? That is his kingdom.

For example, imagine a large, sprawling empire ruled by a monarchy. The old king has been recently deposed, and a new king has come to power. This new king is loved by some of its citizens but hated by others. While some of the citizens do what the king wishes and desires, there are still pockets of resistance, where citizens rebel. In this illustration, we see the two aspects of the kingdom at work.

The king has the sovereign *right to rule* the entire empire. Thus, the entire empire is his kingdom. But in practical terms, *only in those places and people where the will of the king is being expressed* is his true kingdom being represented. Those true and loyal subjects in the kingdom, expressing the will of the king, might be grieved by the pockets of rebellion and resistance they see around them. They might even want to cry out, "Stop this rebellion! Let the will of the king be done!" This is exactly the kind of prayer Jesus taught the subjects of his kingdom to pray:

> "This, then, is how you should pray: "'Our Father in heaven, hallowed be your name, your kingdom come, your will be done on earth as it is in heaven."
> --Matt. 6:9, 10

In this prayer, the subjects of the kingdom are taught to pray to the King for his rule (i.e., his kingdom) to come to earth.

"...as it is in heaven." --Mt. 6:10

In heaven, both aspects of God's kingdom are perfectly expressed. We know, of course, God has the *right to rule* in heaven. Heaven is his throne (Isa. 66:1). Not only does he have the right to rule in heaven, but *he does rule* heaven. Every being in heaven comes under his rule and reign. There is perfect harmony in heaven, because heaven is populated with angels and saints--those who delight to do the will of their King.

Earth is a different story. On earth, we find some factors that dramatically affect the extent of God's kingdom expressed. First of all, on earth there is another kingdom, an opposing kingdom attempting to be extended by an evil impostor called the devil. And secondly, the people of earth, as in the previous illustration, are not all equally excited about being subject to the rule of the King. It started in the garden of Eden, where the deception of satan (and Adam and Eve's subsequent disobedience to God) allowed the devil to have access to a place of rule not intended for him. God had told Adam and Eve the way the rule of the kingdom worked:

> "Then God said, 'Let us make man in our image, in our likeness, and let them rule over the fish of the sea and the birds of the air, over the livestock, over all the earth, and over all the creatures that move along the ground.' So God created man in his own image, in the image of God he created him; male and female he created them. God blessed them and said to them, 'Be fruitful and increase in number; fill the earth and subdue it. Rule over the fish of the sea and the birds of the air and over every living creature that moves on the ground.'" --Gen. 1:27-28

In effect, God said, "I'll rule over you as your King. And as my son and daughter, I've delegated authority to you to rule on earth over the rest of creation." Before the fall of Adam and Eve, satan and his demons existed, but they had no legal right to rule anything or anyone. They had been banished from heaven, where God's perfect rule would not allow them to stay, and satan had no way to expand his power base, his rule, his 'kingdom.' He had first tried to expand it in heaven:

> "How you have fallen from heaven, O morning star, son of the dawn! You have been cast down to the earth, you who once laid low the nations! You said in your heart, 'I will ascend to heaven; I will raise my throne above the stars of God; I will sit enthroned on the mount of assembly, on the utmost heights of the sacred mountain. I will ascend above

the tops of the clouds; I will make myself like the Most High.' But you are brought down to the grave, to the depths of the pit." --Isaiah 14:12-15

Since satan was banished from residency in heaven, he had no choice but to look for some way to rule on earth. Only one thing in God's creation on earth had been given freedom to choose or not choose God: people. This was his only chance. With cunning strategy, satan tricked Adam and Eve into temporarily looking to him as their king instead of God. The results were catastrophic.

Ever since, we find two kingdoms clashing on earth. The evidence of these clashing kingdoms is somewhat veiled in the Old Testament. We get a brief picture of the clash in the book of Job, where satan is allowed to bring affliction onto one of the subjects of God's kingdom. Only a few other places other than the first two chapters of Job is satan even mentioned by name (cf. 1 Chronicles 21:1 and Zechariah 3:1-2).

In the New Testament, however, we see a very visible kingdom clash happening as soon as Jesus Christ enters the scene. 62 of the 76 times 'satan' or 'devil' appears in the Bible occur after the Son of God appears on planet earth. In particular, the devil shows up first in the New Testament to tempt Jesus in the wilderness as He was fasting for forty days. This is nothing less than an assault of the enemy against the Kingdom rule of our God. And so it has gone for thousands of years, this clash of kingdoms.

Because of Jesus' marvelous atoning sacrifice, the victory is already won, of course, and we know how it all ends. But until the second coming of Christ, we have the work of expanding His rule (kingdom) everywhere we go. We are pushing back darkness--the gates of hell cannot prevail--and we are advancing His kingdom.

The Centrality Of The Kingdom

This is no peripheral message. The kingdom of God is central to our purpose and mission as the people of God. The word "church" is referenced 79 times and only in the New Testament, while the word "kingdom" occurs in both Old and New Testaments nearly 300 times in the Scriptures. More importantly than frequency of occurrences, though, is the centrality of the kingdom. The word "church" is often used in a cursory or passing way ("Greet the church in their house."), or it is used to reference the larger body of Christ. The word "kingdom" occupies amazing centrality in the Scriptures. Let's look at a few examples of how central the kingdom is in New Testament Christianity:

Jesus modeled the centrality of the kingdom. The kingdom was Jesus' first and continual message (Mk. 1:15; Mat. 4:17). He went throughout Galilee preaching the good news of the kingdom and healing the sick (Mt. 4:23). In the beatitudes, he consoled people with the kingdom (Mt. 5:3-10). Jesus loved to talk about the kingdom, likening it to wise virgins, a wedding banquet, a vineyard, a king settling accounts, a net, a pearl of great price, a treasure in a field, a farmer sowing seed, a mustard seed, and yeast. At one point, Jesus said that He was compelled to preach about the kingdom, because that is why He was sent (Lk. 4:43). Jesus spoke to the crowds about the kingdom of God (Lk. 9:11), going from one town and village to another (Lk. 8:1). After His resurrection and before His ascension, Jesus' final message was to speak for 40 days about the kingdom of God (Acts 1:3).

The early church learned the centrality of the kingdom. Jesus taught his disciples to pray for the kingdom to come (Mt. 6:10). He sent them out with the message of the kingdom (Lk. 9:2). Jesus conferred on his disciples the kingdom (Lk. 22:29) and told them to sacrifice and go to the mission field for the sake of the kingdom of God (Lk. 18:29). Philip preached the good news of the kingdom of God and the name of Jesus Christ (Acts 8:12). Paul taught on the kingdom of God over a three-month period (Acts 19:8) and declared the kingdom of God from morning until evening to lost people (Acts 28:23). He boldly declared the kingdom (Acts 28:31), and Paul said that he and his fellow workers were working for the kingdom of God (Col. 4:11). Paul charged Timothy to fulfill his ministry in light of the kingdom (2 Tim. 4:1).

The church's primary ministry activity is the kingdom! God's kingdom resides within believers by the Holy Spirit (Lk. 17:20-21). The kingdom is not about food, but about righteousness, peace, and joy in the Holy Spirit (Rom. 14:17). We are called into His kingdom and glory (1 Th. 2:12). The Father is pleased to give us the kingdom (Lk.. 12:32). The kingdom of God belongs to people with childlikeness (Mt. 18:3; Lk. 18:16). Our inheritance is an unshakeable kingdom of light (Col. 1:12; Heb. 12:28), and we have been made a kingdom of priests (Rev. 1:6; 5:10). We have been given the knowledge of the secrets of the kingdom (Lk. 8:10), and to not understand the message of the kingdom means that the enemy has been at work (Mt. 13:19). We've been given the keys of the kingdom to bind and loose (Mt. 16:19), and deliverance from demons is an evidence of the kingdom (Lk. 11:20). The essence of God's kingdom does not consist of words, but of power (1 Cor. 4:20). Before Christ returns, the gospel of the kingdom will be preached in every nation (Mt. 24:14). We are told to seek first the kingdom of God (Mt. 6:33).

Kingdom First, Church Second

To build churches with kingdom *eyes*, then, means that we build the church with peripheral vision. Did you know God never asked us to *focus* on the church? Jesus has always maintained that He would build the church! (Mt. 16:18). He asked us to focus on His kingdom by seeking it first (Mt. 6:33). Church was always meant to be a byproduct of the kingdom of God. The church is the community of the kingdom, not the kingdom itself. As we give ourselves to the expansion of God's kingdom, from giving a glass of cold water in Jesus' name to a thirsty child from the neighborhood, to prophesying at the convenience store to a patron, to preaching a sermon, to mowing our neighbors' lawn, to praying for healing for our sick cousin, we are expanding God's kindness (and therefore His rule) wherever we go. Because God is so amazingly beautiful, people are attracted to Him. As a result, they want to hang out with you and others who embody this kingdom. This community of kingdom people is called the church, and pretty soon, the church flourishes, all because we put the kingdom first.

Scripture explains that some realities only operate through other dynamics. For example, we know that faith works through love (Gal. 5:6). In other words, only in the context of the love of God can the faith of God really operate, flourish, and find true expression. Faith just doesn't work in solitude, as an "orphan." It must be accompanied by and preceded by love. 1 Corinthians 13 tells us that the kind of powerful faith that can move mountains amounts to nothing without the love of God coursing through it.

In the same way, church only "works" *through* the lens of the kingdom. It is vital that those who are engaged in the enterprise of church are wearing kingdom lenses. Our desire for a glorious, radiant church (Eph. 5:27) is right. Our desire for excellence in the building process (1 Cor. 3:10) is also right. A kingdom lens helps us to remain "friends of the Bridegroom" (Jn. 3:29) and to remember that "the bride belongs to the Bridegroom." We are to present a glorious, radiant church to *Him*, not to ourselves.

REDEFINING SUCCESS

If church leaders and all God's people could digest these truths and really walk them out, we would be on our way to a revolution. I deeply appreciate the church growth movement and see it as a gift from God that helped us get over ourselves and focus on lost people. However, we are capable of misusing the gifts of God, and I believe we have done so with the issue of church growth.

In some ways, a kingdom church functions exactly opposite of a church steeped in church growth principles. Many of our churches are founded upon principles that are self-serving and competitive. The principles of the kingdom are revolutionary. The way up is down. The greatest among us will become a servant of all. Just think if we applied these truths to our local churches. Churches out serving one another! Churches not feeling jealous but joyful when another church down the street grows faster than itself. Churches not so quick to promote their own name. Churches that share resources. Pastors that moved from the fear of stealing sheep to the fear of possessing sheep!

One of my favorite people is Steve Sjogren, founder of Vineyard Community Church in Cincinnati, Ohio. Some years ago, Steve initiated a weekly "ServeFest" on Saturday mornings at the church, where a bunch of people regularly practiced "servant evangelism", the art of doing small things with great love. For example, they would give away free sodas on a hot day and attach a small church business card to the can. I remember hearing how Steve and the church had been so ridiculously successful at this outreach ministry that they decided to do some of their outreaches and put *another church's name* on the business card instead of their own. That is a great example of a kingdom church in action.

One of Steve's slogans is "kindness with no strings attached." This is what it means to be a kingdom church, and this is how God defines success. It is not irresponsible to be free from hidden motives. It is Christlike.

The Problem With Success

I am pro-success. I really enjoy succeeding much more than failing! Success is not a problem, but our understanding of success can be problematic. Appearances can be quite deceiving, which is perhaps one reason why Paul exhorted us not to compare ourselves with each other (2 Cor. 10:12). For example, Jesus was guilty of "shrinking" the church. In John 6, after sharing quite an interesting discourse about eating his flesh and drinking his blood with his listeners, pretty much the entire "preChristian" crowd he had gathered left. Sadly, some of our definitions of success would have forced us to categorize Jesus as a failure.

Some years ago, my wife and I and our three daughters moved across the country to plant a church from scratch. Without a team, on a wing and a prayer, God gave us great grace to move to a brand-new city and start a church. I was very anxious to see the church grow, and after 6 months, we started our first Sunday morning service with about 70 people. We were excited, and we were certain it was onward and upward from there. Soon I would be able to quit my job as a part-time TV salesman and devote myself fully to "the ministry." Little did I know that God would interrupt my plans with a "John 6" word. He spoke to my heart: "Mark, I want you to help some people 'hop off the bus.'" Startled, I said, "Lord, what do you mean?" I sensed Him say, "In your effort to grow the church, you've gathered some people who aren't meant to be here, and I want you to say and do some things that will help them move on to another church."

This was a difficult word to hear. It ran against everything I had been taught. It would make me look bad, perhaps even appearing as a failure or a flake to those who were aware of my efforts to plant a church. It was going to cost something financially as well. We were running out of money both personally and as a church, and I really couldn't *afford* to obey this word and lose tithing members! And how would I explain it to my wife?

In the end, God won, my ego lost, and I have never regretted obeying Him! I did, in fact, say and do some things that caused the church to drop to about half its size. I sensed the pleasure of the Lord. Two really great things happened as a result of this act of obedience. First, my family and I had our first real experience of supernatural provision. That winter, we ran out of money, but without asking anybody or putting out a newsletter, we received financial help in the mail, sometimes from people who didn't even know us personally. We had the awesome privilege of watching God provide for us. Second, God began teaching me about His definition of success.

Success Is Obedience

Success in the kingdom is defined by one word: *obedience.*

> "To obey is better than sacrifice, and to heed is better than the fat of rams." --1 Sam. 15:22

Obedience sometimes works in your favor, and sometimes it just plain costs you. But obedience is how God defines success in kingdom churches. Over the years I have interacted with hundreds of pastors. It is amazing how many conversations have been redirected around to the topic of church size, number of small groups, etc. It often demonstrates the lack of kingdom thinking in many leaders. Success defined as obedience does not excuse poor quality, laziness, inwardness, nor does it legitimize unwise practices in the name of God's leading. I have worked very hard to be smart in how we've administrated our responsibilities before God and man. We have sought to win the lost, to build infrastructure, and to do things that demonstrate wisdom and produce fruitfulness. But what I am saying is that obedience transcends all these other things, and if we're not careful, we can easily apply wrong standards in a superficial way that devalue the kingdom and inadvertently promote a value of self-preservation in churches.

I have found that some pastors really just need to go start businesses! Often pastors have an entrepreneurial bent and a desire to create something that they can be proud of. This is a good thing! They have a strong desire for success, but like blood from a turnip, they are trying to squeeze feelings of success from the church. Everyone can feel this underlying tone, and the people feel that they are being subtly used to help the leaders feel successful. We've gotten so used to it in church culture that we can hardly imagine what it might feel like to have an absence of opportunism in the leadership of the church.

And, of course, it's not simply the leaders. Many people join churches and join ministries in order to gain feelings of success and legitimacy. But the church is not the right place to feed insecurities and the need for outward success. It is a place to come, lay down your life, and die among a house of friends all doing the same thing!

A passage of Scripture that has particular meaning for me is John 12:24-25:

> "I tell you the truth, unless a kernel of wheat falls to the ground and dies, it remains only a single seed. But if it dies, it produces many seeds. The man who loves his life will lose it, while the man who hates his life in this world will keep it for eternal life."

On the same occasion where we moved across the country to plant a church, this is the Scripture that God spoke to my heart before we made the decision to go. We were pastoring a newer, growing, vibrant church in a beautiful area of California. Life was good. Our church family was close, and the vibe of the church was positive. The Holy Spirit was moving in power, people were receiving Christ, and there were many other aspects to the church that we were so thankful for. People in our denomination were beginning to take notice of what was happening in our church, and I was well-positioned for a successful career in ministry! In the middle of it all, God spoke to our hearts and invited us to lay it all down, to give it all away, to move to relative obscurity in a declining, economically challenged city in the Midwest. His call was this: "Come and die!" One guy I spoke with put it like this: "God wants to kill you so He can use you."

I strongly agree with those who advocate staying in one location for a number of years--if that's what you're called to. However, Jesus and Paul would not be part of the "longevity club", because they had other kinds of mandates from God:

> "At daybreak Jesus went out to a solitary place. The people were looking for him and when they came to where he was, *they tried to keep him from leaving them.* But he said, 'I must preach the good news of the kingdom of God to the other towns also, because that is why I was sent.'" -- Lk. 4:42-43

Paul was a church planting apostle who did his work during a series of three missionary journeys. He often wasn't around long enough at a given church to even appoint elders.

Fact is, we're not building a career. I love what John Wimber used to say: "I don't have a ministry. There is only one ministry, and it's His ministry. I am entering into His ministry." Kingdom churches are built by kingdom people who don't own anything in ministry. This is a hard truth. A.W. Tozer, in his book, The Pursuit Of God, calls this *"The Blessedness Of Possessing Nothing."* This is the call of God to every kingdom church and kingdom leader: an open hand and a loose grip.

CULTIVATING RIGHT MOTIVATION

My encouragement to all of us desiring to see the church come into her destiny in this day and time is to go before

God continually for a right heart, especially those of us in America who have been influenced by a culture of image and success. David prayed in Psalm 51, "Create in me a clean heart, O God."

I don't mean introspectively examining ourselves and becoming overly concerned with our motives in a way that produces anxiety. However, Scripture makes it clear that our motives are examined and tested by the Lord, and frankly, *godly motivation is at the core of building kingdom churches.* People with wrong motives can't build right churches--no matter how successful they may look on the outside. In gathering materials for Solomon to build the temple, David spoke aloud about his motivation and the process by which God examines us:

> "I know, my God, that you test the heart and are pleased
> with integrity." --1 Chronicles 29:17

We cannot get free from false motivations by focusing on them. We can only become free as we have a greater motivation that pales lesser ones. Jesus explained this principle in John 5:44:

> "How can you believe, when you receive glory from one
> another and you do not seek the glory that is from the one
> and only God?" (NASB)

I believe that a continual pursuit of the glory of God that includes resting in His love for us (Zeph. 3:17) and desiring to please Him more and more (1 Thess. 4:1) is essential to building kingdom churches. As God is raising up new kinds of churches with a new wave of leaders, we want to make sure that we don't simply latch on to strategy and structure and miss the heart of it all (Lk. 11:39).

Three Keys To Kingdom Motivation

Jesus wants His church back. If Jesus is going to be the functional Head of His church, for real, that means the rest of us are going to need to take a step down, a demotion, lower than before. This is not a time to promote ourselves or our ministries, because the Father is looking to promote His Son, exclusively.

In Ezekiel 16, the LORD uses Jeremiah to confront His people with three dominant sins of the people then and of us now:

> "Now this was the sin of your sister Sodom: She and her daughters were *arrogant*, *overfed*, and *unconcerned*; they did not help the poor and needy." --Ezekiel 16:49

The antidote for arrogance is *humility*, for being overfed is *hunger*, and for being unconcerned is *holiness*. There is a doorway standing open in heaven (Rev. 4:1), but it is small and low, just able to be passed through by those on their knees. On the other side of this doorway is revival, revolution, joy unspeakable and full of glory. All the resources of heaven are on the other side of this doorway. But the only people that will fit through this doorway are ones who are marked by these three traits of humility, hunger, and holiness. These are the riches of all those involved in revival.

Humility. There is an *invitation to humility* happening in the church in the West. For years, we have thought of ourselves more highly than we ought. While other parts of the world have been experiencing great revival, God has bypassed much of the church in the West in order to reveal to us where we're really at and to provoke us to jealousy. Humility attracts God's presence and releases God's promises in our lives. Francis Frangipane says that humility is the armor of heaven. It is the dividing line between faith and presumption. It keeps us safe from the many difficulties associated with arrogance and pride. Humility is much more profound than honesty about our problems or looking at the ground when we speak. It's about dependency and childlike trust and doesn't contain a whiff of self-righteousness or defensiveness. Jesus declared Himself to be humble of heart (Mt. 11:28-30). This is where God is taking the church, because humility is absolutely essential in order to walk in the kind of power and authority God desires to release in His church.

> "God resists the proud but gives grace to the humble." --Jms. 4:6

Hunger. There is also an *invitation to hunger* happening in the church. Desire for God's person, His presence, His provision and His power are growing in this hour. Did you know that hunger in our culture is actually a miracle? It's one thing to be hungry when you're in the middle of the desert and you don't own anything but the clothes on your back. You don't know where you're going, where your next meal is coming from, and you're like a dependent child. This can create hunger! People who live today in countries where food and basic necessities are in short supply, they are prone to understand the need for hunger for God! But much of the West is a land of abundance. Where I live, in the Central Coast of California, with beautiful weather, vineyards, orchards, ranches, farms, retirement accounts, nice vehicles, nice church buildings, tidy sermons, sweet worship, great sound systems, good friends, great soccer teams for our kids, fun vacations, coffee shops and convenience stores just for us...where does hunger fit with that? Sustained hunger is a miracle here and in many places in the Western church! But God is granting it as a gift to those who will embrace hunger and all that it means.

"Blessed are those who hunger and thirst for righteousness, for they shall be filled." --Mt. 5:8

Holiness. Finally, there is a gracious *invitation to holiness* in the church in the West. This is good news for every sincere believer who has felt stuck in patterns of sinful impurity. God is extending high levels of grace for the Bride is to "make herself ready" for the wedding feast of the Lamb. Yes, holiness is a choice made by each believer, empowered by God's grace. Psalm 29:2 says, "Worship the LORD in the beauty of holiness." It is as we engage the beautiful God that we find issues of holiness easier to walk out. Millions of believers are now rediscovering or discovering for the first time the majestic beauty of the Lord Jesus Christ and the deep love of the Father, and the result is great freedom from sinful patterns that previously bound them. The definition of holiness is *"being pure in heart and life, set apart for God's purpose."* Holiness means becoming more like Jesus and being wholly given to God as His very own possession. As we rest in His ability to bring about holiness in our lives, we experience the victory that was already purchased for us over time:

"I, the Lord, am holy, and I *make* you holy."
                                        --Lev. 21:8 (NLT)

Holiness is expressed not only in purity of lifestyle but also in purity of religion (Jms. 1:27). We walk free from the spirit of Sodom when we help the poor and needy. A life of love has to become tangible. Someone I know and deeply respect says it this way: "Love has to look like something." Holiness is demonstrated as we give ourselves to others. Lesser things fade away among a people in love, first with God, and then with the people they are serving.

Let Us Pray

In the following chapters, we will review more strategic elements of building kingdom churches, but none of it makes any sense if our hearts don't own kingdom motivation. God is raising up a people with the right heart and the right motivation. His eyes are looking throughout the earth for those wholehearted, kingdom people filled with humility, hunger, and holiness. My prayer is that you and I will cultivate kingdom motivation through a life of prayer filled with intimacy with God. Let's be a generation postured before the throne of God so that He can have access to our hearts and change us from glory to glory.

> *"Father, I invite you to bring your Divine searchlight and reveal motivation in me that is self-serving. I deeply desire to be a kingdom person with wholehearted love for you and a generous spirit toward others. Take every part of me! Release the refining fire of your Presence on my heart. I want to be completely free from lesser motivations. Fill me with your definitions of success. I embrace humility, hunger, and holiness as success in You. Amen."*

Chapter Three
Kingdom INTENSITY

"...the kingdom of heaven has endured violent assault, and violent men seize it by force [as a precious prize]--a share in the heavenly kingdom is sought for with *most ardent zeal* and *intense exertion.*" --Mt. 11:12, Amplified

Closely related to motivation is intensity. The strength and purity of our motivation has direct impact on the quality and degree of our intensity. When the motivations of heaven wash over our hearts again and again, the intensity with which we build the kingdom of God is exponentially increased.

Building kingdom churches requires intensity, because intensity is a Biblical trait of the King and all those who are radically pursuing His kingdom. Kingdom churches are made up of people who possess an inward quality of divine intensity. This intensity is not related to personality. It has to do with ardent desire birthed from a heart of love. The fruit of intimacy with God is intensity. And this Biblical intensity, as described in Matthew 11 and other places, has to do with "most ardent zeal" and "intense exertion." Intensity from God's perspective is more than optional. It is necessary for the kind of people and churches He desires to build. While our God has always appreciated and reproduced intensity in the hearts of His people, the church in the West is just starting to have a fresh appreciation for His intensity.

FIRE

Fire is a Biblical metaphor for kingdom intensity. Since the Pentecostal movement originated in the early 1900s, there has been a fairly sustained emphasis in much of the church on the doctrine and practice of the baptism of the Holy Spirit. However, much of the church in the West has missed part of the promise. In Luke 3:16, John the Baptist states the full promise: "I baptize you with water. But one more powerful than I will come...He will baptize you with the Holy Spirit *and with fire.*"

This baptism of fire has been largely relegated in our thinking to the idea of suffering and refinement. Surely the metaphor of fire in the Scriptures has to do with these things. But the context of John's statement was with reference to power and internal burning. Someone more powerful than me is coming, John said, and the net result is that people will experience immersion in fire. Intensity is related to an inward burning released from the God of fire Himself. This inward fire is none other than God dwelling in the human heart. The inward fire that God provides is so powerful that it terrifies sinners and calls to saints as a holy invitation to a spirit of continual burning:

> "Sinners in Zion are terrified; trembling has seized the godless. 'Who among us can live with *the consuming fire? Who among us can live with continual burning?'"* --Isa. 33:14

Notice that 'the consuming fire' is God Himself! (Heb. 12:29) There is an invitation to dwell continually with this God of fire. The result will be a continual burning in our own hearts and lives.

The God Of Fire

There are about 450 references to fire in the Scripture. When Hebrews 12:29 says that our God is a consuming fire, this is not simply a description of His judgments or refinements, but it is a description of His essence and His nature. In nearly every major encounter in the Scriptures where someone saw the Lord, God purposely chose to reveal Himself in a way that involved fire. Moses' first exposure to God was the angel of the Lord that appeared to Moses in the midst of the burning bush (Ex. 3:2). The Israelites saw God's glory, and it looked to them like a consuming fire (Ex. 24:17). In Gideon's encounter with the Lord, fire sprang up from the rock and consumed Gideon's sacrifice (Judges 6:21). At the dedication of the temple, after Solomon had prayed, fire came down from heaven and consumed the sacrifices, and God's glory filled the place (2 Chr. 7:1). When Elijah confronted the false prophets of Baal, he boldly declared, "the God who answers by fire, He is God." (1 Kings 18:24). Later, the fire of the Lord fell and consumed the burnt offering and everything around it (v. 38). When Isaiah saw the Lord, the temple was filled with smoke and the altar of fire was the source of the coal that touched his lips and unlocked his heart (Isa. 6:6). In Ezekiel's introductory vision of the Lord and His dwelling place, fire and brilliant flashes of light were constant. Ezekiel tried to describe the Lord in two categories of "waist up and waist down", but in the end, they were both descriptions of fire!

> "Then I noticed form the appearance of His loins and upward something like glowing metal that looked like fire all around within it, and from the appearance of His loins and downward I saw something like fire; and there was a radiance around Him." --Ez. 1:27

It continues like this throughout Scripture. Daniel's three friends walked with a fourth Man in the midst of fire (Dan. 3:25). The early church received tongues of fire (Acts 2:3). Paul says Jesus will return in "blazing fire with his powerful angels" (2 Th. 1:7). Even in Revelation, John tells us that the Son of Man had eyes like flames of fire and a face that was burning with brilliant light (Rev. 1:14-16). One of the primary manifestations of the God of Heaven is through the reality of burning fire.

It is a universal human reaction to enjoy and embrace the kindnesses and mercies of God. But the human reaction to this God of fire is illustrated when Moses recounted to the Israelites their own reaction to the fiery God:

> "The LORD spoke to you face to face at the mountain in the midst of the fire, while I was standing between the LORD and you at the time...for *you were afraid because of the fire and did not go up the mountain.*" --Deut. 5:4-5

Many years ago, my wife had a vision of myriads of people stretched along the California coastline, lined up on the beach facing the ocean, waiting for a tidal wave to come. It was a wave of refreshing and joy, and the people were eager to receive it. And then, intense, fiery lights of amber, blue and other colors began to shoot up from behind the wave. These lights of fire represented the awesome power and the glory of God, and the people were greatly afraid. Many wanted the wave of refreshing, but fewer wanted the fire. Our God is a consuming fire, and He will baptize us with the Holy Spirit and with fire.

For decades, we have had meetings to release the baptism of the Spirit. This is a good thing! I went to such a meeting in 1977, and I received the baptism of the Spirit! My life was radically touched and changed. The sky was bluer, and the grass was greener! Over the years, I have also grown to appreciate the fire of God and the need for believers to experience the baptism of fire. Today, the fire of God is being released, and it is exposing and refining our hearts. It is an awesome and holy reality that the God of heaven is literally sharing His own nature with us by releasing a baptism of fire. Fire cleanses, purifies, and empowers.

Fire Is The Issue

Fire has always been a dividing line. While we are often quick to blame the structure of the church for ruling over people and not releasing the priesthood of all believers, our shallow analysis misses the root problem. It is not primarily the fault of leadership that the priesthood of all believers has been inactive. It is the fear of drawing close to the God of fire that resides in each of our own hearts. We shrink back, just like the Israelites, and we feel much safer allowing a representative to draw close to God while we keep a safe distance from Him.

The story in Exodus 19 dramatically illustrates this point. In Exodus 19, we find God joyously communicating a message to His people through Moses the prophet. The message is about His own love and desire for His people. He explains that the way each person can experience this God of fiery desire is to walk in the role of individual priest before the Lord (Ex. 19:6). The people hear this invitation of love, and their hearts say "yes!" They tell the Lord that they agree to this kind of loving, individual relationship with Him as priests (Ex. 19:8).

After this, the Lord exhorts the people to consecrate themselves and not to act presumptuously by ascending the mountain of the Lord in a careless way. His invitation to relationship is not diminished by His strong call to consecration. They are commensurate. In the midst of His instructions, God says, "When you hear the long blast of the ram's horn, then come up the mountain." (19:13) By inviting His people up the mountain with Moses, the Lord literally welcomes each Israelite into the same kind of closeness that previously only Moses had enjoyed with God. Moses himself is confused. He objects to the Lord, saying, "The people cannot come up to Mount Sinai, for You warned us!" (19:23). But God just ignores Moses and tells him to remind the people not to be presumptuous. These restrictions are not meant to keep God's people from relationship, but rather He is testing them in issues of consecration (20:20).

Then one of the most tragic events in the history of Israel occurs. God's people "refuse Him who is speaking." They had clearly heard God's heart of love through Moses and His invitation into direct relationship. They said "yes!" to times of refreshing. But when they encounter the God of fire, He is so overwhelmingly powerful that they opt out of closeness. God expresses Himself with great passion and desire through fire, smoke, divine shaking and the loud sound of a heavenly trumpet. This was their cue to come close and to ascend the mountain of the Lord, each of them! It is an amazing moment in history. Their first reaction is to tremble--an appropriate reaction indeed! But their inappropriate level of fear (v. 20) causes them to misinterpret God's actions. As a result, they subtly reject God and miss out on the direct relationship He had just invited them into and they had just agreed to!

> "All the people *perceived* the thunder and the lightning flashes and the sound of the trumpet and the mountain smoking; and *when* the people saw it, they trembled and *stood at a distance.* Then they said to Moses, *'Speak to us yourself* and we will listen; *but let not God speak to us,* or we will die.'" --Ex. 20:18-19

The people choose a mediated relationship rather than individual closeness with the living God. After the people's decision to not walk as priests, the Lord no longer invited them up the mountain into closeness. He accepted their decision.

The God Of Fiery Desire

There is something about fire that pleases the Lord. The entire system of sacrificial offerings was based on fire (Lev. 23:25). This issue of fire is more than a metaphor. Fire can represent many things in the Scriptures--purity, refinement, judgment, testing, light, and so on. But central in the metaphor of fire is the expression of fiery desire. I believe fire is precious to God because it speaks of the strength of His desire for us and of the appropriate kind of intense response in our hearts towards Him. Fire means burning, and the love of God burns in His own heart toward us! He desires a people of fire who burn with the same fire that is in His heart.

Though we now live under the New Covenant, this fiery God remains intensely focused on intimate relationship with His people. Jesus gives us a glimpse of the burning in His own heart when He says to His disciples, "I have *earnestly and intensely desired* to eat this Passover with you" (Luke 22:14, AMP). What an amazingly strong statement over a meal! But this meal, at the culmination of His time of ministry here on earth, represented an intimate, uninterrupted time of relationship with His friends. The same Greek word used here is translated in other places as 'longing', 'yearning', and 'lust.' And the words in the Greek, *epithumia* and *epithumio*, are used back to back to indicate the strength of desire in the heart of the Lord Jesus. The KJV has trouble giving proper and culturally acceptable English words to this expression by Jesus, so it gets tongue-tied and says, "With desire I have desired..." We have similar trouble today fully grasping the intensity in the heart of God for us. He is longing with intense desire to be close to us, to have relationship with us, and as His image is formed in us and we become more and more Christlike, we will, without exception, grow in fiery intensity, just like Him.

ZEAL

The appropriate response to a God of fire is zeal. Zeal is a gift from God that creates the kind of intensity needed to become a kingdom people who extend God's kingdom and build kingdom churches. They cannot be built apart from holy zeal.

"The zeal of the LORD will accomplish this." --2 Ki. 19:31

Because zeal comes from God, it is not dependent on a type 'A' personality. It is not hype, nor is it manufactured. This zeal is the inward burning of the Holy Spirit released in the human heart that provides supernatural motivation and intensity. Because zeal is a command, you do not need a certain personality type to walk with Jesus and feel fire on the inside. You may have a personality that is as cool as a cucumber, very phlegmatic in your approach to life. But as you lay back in your emotional Easy-boy recliner, and the Holy Spirit begins to speak to You, it feels like fire on the inside! And you find yourself saying, "Wow. This is the God of fire. He is dealing with me, and I will respond with zeal for Him!" When the disciples spoke with Jesus on the road to Emmaus, they immediately testified of an encounter with fire: "Did not our hearts burn within us?" (Lk. 24:32)

> "Never be lacking in zeal, but keep your spiritual fervor,
> serving the Lord." --Rom. 12:11

Zechariah prophesied that God's purposes are accomplished not by the might or power of man, but rather by the Spirit of God. Jesus called us to an easy burden and a light yoke. This is key. The more we come in contact with the God of fire and fiery desire, the more that divine zeal is released in us. As we experience the love of God, we find that it burns in us and changes everything.

John the Baptist was a "burning and shining light" who carried an internal zeal unlike any other in his generation. But John's zeal was to be the 'norm' among the people of the kingdom! (Mt. 11:11).

Zeal is much more than a personality trait. It is the heart of God growing in us, providing internal fire and motivation beyond our human resources. The Greek word for zeal comes from the root word "zeo" which means "*to be hot, to boil, to glow, to be fervent*." Jesus expressed this kind of zeal when he turned over the tables of the money changers. Zeal (i.e., ardent desire and jealousy) for the place where the Father dwelt was a complete preoccupation for Jesus (John

2:17). He so loved His Father that His internal fire was commensurate with His love. This is to be the nature of the church, motivated by ardent desire for the Father's dwelling place on earth. To be motivated for lesser things, like growing a church, will easily burn people out. But being motivated by love has a uniquely sustaining dynamic.

Free From Burnout

When we walk with the beautiful Son of God, we walk in the midst of fire, and yet, like the burning bush, we are not consumed. Like Shadrach, Meshach, and Abednego, we find ourselves in the midst of fire with the Son of Man, unbound, unharmed and we don't even smell like smoke (Dan. 3:25-27).

Many people are afraid to live in the place of zeal, lest they burn out. But this is a misconception. Jeremiah tried to go this route of calming himself down and being reasonable. He tried to deny the internal zeal of God that was his normal motivation.

> "...if I say, 'I will not mention him or speak any more in his name,' his word is in my heart like a fire, a fire shut up in my bones. I am weary of holding it in; indeed, I cannot.'"
>
> --Jer. 20:9

God-authored zeal has divine energy attached to it. People in love don't burn out. Oh, they may tire, and yes, they may need to take some time off to rest. But crash and burn? No. They don't. They can't. The internal fire of love is too strong. You may think this is an idealistic notion, or perhaps, as someone who has burned out before, you may even feel insulted. But we mustn't reduce our theology to make up for where our experience is lacking.

> "Love is as strong as death...it burns like blazing fire, like a mighty flame. Many waters cannot quench love; rivers cannot wash it away." --Song of Songs 8:6-7

The power of love is clear and compelling. It is stronger than death. It burns like a blazing fire, like a mighty flame. Many waters cannot quench it, and rivers cannot wash it away. Can you burn out with such love? No. You cannot. *Love never fails.* Burnout is not caused by hard work, although working too much can contribute to the conditions that lead to burnout. Burnout is caused by doing things without the internal fuel to do them, doing the wrong things over a period of time without the internal sustaining life and motivation of the love of God, performing for people's approval rather than laboring in love. A people in love don't burn out, because there is a built-in safeguard. People in love with God obey God, and they will not give themselves to activities that are not in God's heart for them to do. When they do, they are close enough to God that He can easily communicate to them, and they will hear a voice behind them, saying, "This is the way; walk in it." Continual rest is available to those who "cease from their own works" (Heb. 4:10). This rest is easily available to a people in love. When you are in love, you have nothing to prove and nothing to fear, so you are not motivated by false things (which leads to burnout).

In John 4, Jesus took the disciples by surprise when he explained to them that he had food they were not aware of. The disciples had gone off to another town, while Jesus remained to converse with the Samaritan woman at the well. Even though his stomach may have been growling before they left, by the time they returned, he had received supernatural sustenance from heaven, so much so that he just told the guys, "Hey, I'm really not hungry, because I was fed by My Father as I was doing His will." In the same way, the love of God 'feeds us' even as we are engaged in the enterprise of His kingdom.

Wake Up

It is not only the job of the enemy to get us to sin, but it is also (and perhaps primarily) the work of the enemy to get us *numb.* If he can succeed in getting the church to not feel and to not care, to be devoid of internal zeal and fiery desire, he has been as successful as if we all entered into deep, dark sin. Why? Because numb people who do not feel anything will fall asleep, and falling asleep spiritually has many dangers associated with it. When Eutychus fell asleep during Paul's talk, he broke his neck and died! How the enemy would like the church to do the same thing. When we're asleep, he has freedom to work:

> "Jesus told them another parable: 'The kingdom of heaven is like a man who sowed good seed in his field. But *while everyone was sleeping, his enemy came* and sowed weeds among the wheat, and went away.'"   --Mt. 13:24-25

> "Be self-controlled and *alert*. Your enemy the devil prowls around like a roaring lion looking for someone to devour."
> --1 Pet. 5:8

Spiritual sleep (and sometimes even physical sleep at the wrong times) is a temptation that we are repeatedly warned about. In the garden, when Jesus was praying concerning His appointment with the Cross, He asked His men to stay alert and to pray. Even though they were in a place of great sorrow, and it would normally be understandable to sympathize with them for falling asleep because of their exhaustion, Jesus actually rebukes them and tells them to get up and pray!

> "When he rose from prayer and went back to the disciples, he found them asleep, *exhausted from sorrow.* 'Why are you sleeping?' he asked them. '*Get up and pray* so that you will not fall into temptation.'" --Lk. 22:45-46

How often we coddle and comfort our flesh, foolishly thinking that God is pleased with our desire to pamper ourselves. I am no ascetic, and I believe in taking good care of ourselves, in recreating, and in enjoying life. But there is a subtle place where our desire in the West to enjoy life can easily put us to sleep spiritually. When we wonder at times why we've missed some of God's dealings and why our hearts sometimes lack internal fire, perhaps we've been sleeping through very important times and have not known it!

> "No soldier in active service entangles himself in the affairs of everyday life, so that he may please the one who enlisted him as a soldier." --2 Tim. 2:4

Jesus said, "Behold, I come as a thief! Blessed is he who *stays awake...*" (Rev. 16:15) Jesus strongly warns us stay awake and alert and to not allow ourselves to be sleeping:

> "No one knows about that day or hour, not even the angels in heaven, nor the Son, but only the Father. *Be on guard! Be alert!* You do not know when that time will come. It's like a man going away: He leaves his house and puts his servants in charge, each with his assigned task, and tells the one at the door to keep watch. Therefore *keep watch* because you do not know when the owner of the house will come back--whether in the evening, or at midnight, or when the rooster crows, or at dawn. If he comes suddenly, *do not let him find you sleeping. What I say to you, I say to everyone: 'Watch!'*" --Mk. 13:32-37

'Staying awake' is no small issue in the Scriptures. Paul says plainly in 1 Thess. 5:6, "So then, let us not be like others, who are asleep, but let us be alert and self-controlled." David stirred himself and even spoke to his own soul, "Awake, my soul! Awake, harp and lyre! I will awaken the dawn" (Ps. 27:8). God's people are continually exhorted to wake up and to pay attention!

> "Awake, awake! Rise up, O Jerusalem..."
> --Isa. 51:17 (cf. 52:1)

> "Wake up, O sleeper, rise from the dead, and Christ will shine on you." --Eph. 5:14

Somebody Needs To Protest

The church in the West must challenge a slumbering spirit in our midst. Like Lazarus, Jesus is saying to us, "Come forth!" Our zeal is precious to God. It is a command to walk continually in holy zeal. Anything less must begin to be met with holy protest.

In Isaiah 64, the prophet saw the condition of God's people and the triumph of the adversaries of God, and he cried out for God to tear open the heavens and to release His zealous fire. The cry in Isaiah's heart is commensurate with the fire in God's own heart. He prayed with zeal because He knew a God of zeal. He was dismayed at the people of God for not stirring themselves in a proper way. He knew there was MORE! And He cried out for it with authority. He prayed according to God's will, offering a cry of desire mingled with protest at the lack of fire in God's people.

> "Oh, that You would *rend the heavens* and that You would come down, that the mountains might *quake and flow down* at Your presence--as when *fire kindles* the brushwood and *the fire causes the water to boil*...that the nations may *tremble at Your presence!* When You did terrible things *which we did not expect,* You came down; the mountains *quaked at Your presence.* For from old no one has heard nor perceived by the ear, nor has the eye seen a God besides You, *Who works and shows Himself active on behalf of him who [earnestly] waits for You...*And no one calls on Your name and *awakens and bestirs himself to take and keep hold of You...*"
> --Isa. 64:1-7, AMP

BREAKTHROUGH

Intensity is more than a good concept meant to accommodate the overly zealous people of the church. *Intensity is required.* For advancement in the Christian life, and for complete victory over the enemy, the church *must* walk in kingdom intensity. The church in the West is anemic and yet often unwilling to walk in the level of intensity required for complete victory. Because it is an intangible quality, kingdom intensity is often considered an accessory and not essential. But how essential it is!

I have been in numerous prayer meetings and gatherings where the subject of breakthrough is prayed for and preached. What percentage of believers desire breakthrough in at least one area of their lives? The answer is 100%! Everybody desires breakthrough in one or several areas of intimacy with God, personal growth, relational love, financial blessing, ministry effectiveness, etc. Could it be that intensity, sustained by holy zeal, is a key missing ingredient for breakthrough in the West? Let's look at a few examples of why intensity is needed for breakthrough:

Intensity For Intimacy

Many Christians are aware of the comfort and promise found in Jeremiah 29:11, that God has plans for us to give us a future and a hope. But the verses that follow explain what God hopes will happen when His children understand their future and their hope:

> "Then you will call upon me and come and pray to me, and I will listen to you. You will seek me and find me when you seek me *with all your heart.*" --Jer. 29:12-13

The promise of finding the God of the universe in this and many other Scriptures is directly linked with wholehearted intensity in seeking and searching for God. Intensity in pursuing the Person of God releases intimacy in the Presence of God. We can literally have as much of the Person of God as we *want.* The desire in us becomes intensity in our pursuit of Him, which He responds to.

Intensity For God's Word

Some believers wonder why their lives never get past superficial places of obedience. It is a mystery to many how they can have God speak to them so clearly, or how they can see something in the Scriptures that applies to them directly, or how they can make a commitment to close friends in an accountability group, and yet in spite of all these sincere intentions, turn right around and walk directly into sin and disobedience to God.

But at least one of the secrets of obedience has to do with intensity in obeying God's Word. In the first chapter of his epistle, the apostle James compares two types of believers. The primary difference between the two is their intensity:

> "Do not merely listen to the word, and so deceive yourselves. Do what it says. Anyone who listens to the word but does not do what it says is like a man who looks at his face in a mirror and, after looking at himself, goes away and immediately forgets what he looks like. But the man who *looks intently* into the perfect law that gives freedom, and continues to do this, not forgetting what he has heard, but doing it--he will be blessed in what he does." --Jms. 1:22-25

This word translated "looks intently"--parakupto--is an intentional stopping, leaning in, stooping down, and looking with longing into something. It differentiates the obedient from the casual Christian.

Intensity For Prayer

James 5:16 says that the "earnest prayer of a righteous person has great power and wonderful results" (AMP). The Greek word translated "earnest" is where we get our word "energy." It has to do with effort and intensity! What makes prayer powerful and effective is not necessarily the volume or the length of our prayer. However, you would be hard-pressed to utter prayers of earnest intensity without any energy put into them. This is not the energy of human effort, but it is the working of God in a human heart:

> "To this end I labor, struggling with all his energy, which so powerfully works in me." --Col. 1:29

Intensity In Personal Progress

In both of the letters Paul addressed to his spiritual son, Timothy, we see evidences of Timothy struggling with timidity and even intimidation. Perhaps part of his struggle was rooted in Timothy's personality, or perhaps Timothy was a sensitive soul who received some level of wounding from authority figures in his youth. What we do know for sure is that Paul was continually exhorting young Timothy to be bold, confident, strong, unafraid, and intense! Paul linked intensity in Timothy with his progress when he told him:

> "Take pains with these things; be absorbed in them, so that your progress will be evident to all."
> --1 Tim. 4:15

Intensity For Victory

One of the most stunning passages of Scripture having to do with intensity is found in 2 Kings 13, where the prophet Elisha is about to pronounce a prophetic blessing on Jehoash, the king of Israel. After telling the king that arrows represented the Lord's victory, he told the king to strike the arrows to the ground as a prophetic symbol of Israel's future victory over Aram, their enemy. This was a defining moment, and the king was in the right place at the right time. But he lacked one thing: intensity! He struck the arrows to the ground three times, and even though Elisha didn't specify how many times the king was supposed to strike the ground, it was evident to Elisha (and to the Lord) that the king lacked a certain degree of intensity required for complete victory.

The amount of times the arrows were to be struck to the ground could only be discerned through an intuitive sense and display of intensity. But the king lacked it. As a result, only partial victory was promised.

I am a strong believer in the grace of God. But as believers, we often allow a shallow ethic to creep into our dealings with God. Ever so careful to be people of grace and not a people of works, we sometimes underestimate the need for intensity. While intensity doesn't earn any merit with God, it does unlock partnership with God. Everything has been provided for us through the Cross! We have inherited every spiritual blessing in the heavenly places in Christ, and we have everything we need that pertains to life and godliness! But for complete victory, God requires human effort, born of His Spirit, that is fitting and appropriate to His nature and to the task at hand.

Kingdom intensity is not about a furrowed brow or a serious, no-fun disposition! The joy of the Lord is our strength, and Jesus went with focus and intensity to the Cross because of the joy that was set before Him. Intensity is a wholehearted, leaning forward, adventuresome approach that unlocks fullness. It is about faith-filled focus that accomplishes much! It is living large, but it is more than living large. It is thinking and behaving as though Jesus is worthy of our entire lives and every breath we breathe. More and more, kingdom intensity will characterize the church of the future.

A NEW NORMAL

What is your normal? One of my friends likes to say, "Normal is a setting on the dryer." He means that normal is a relative term. What we normally consider normal on earth may not be normal at all in heaven! We can't look to our contemporaries to define normal for us, because they may not always have a clear grasp on Biblical norms. How true this is when it comes to issues of zeal and fire. We who are part of the church in the West have learned to live with so little, to desire so little, to feel so little, and to have so little internal fire. *But it's not normal!* There is so much more!

> "Eye has not seen, ear has not heard, nor has it entered into the heart of man how much God has prepared for those who love Him." --1 Cor. 2:9

While speaking to the church in Laodicea in Revelation 3, Jesus explained that for Him, normal is that we would be either completely on fire, in love, holy in our behavior and wholly His in our hearts, or that we would be icy in our affections, distant, self-centered and immoral. It was never normal for Jesus to have a majority of His church be simply moral! Being tepid in our Christianity is quite distasteful to the God of fire.

God is redefining normal--not that it ever changed for Him! He is adjusting the default setting in the heart of the Western church from laissez-faire to fire, from 'balanced' in a wrong way to burning in a right way. Passion for God expressed through wholehearted, extravagant devotion and obedience will become the normal Christian experience of the church in the West.

Revivalists

What we are describing is continuous revival. Kingdom churches are made up of people who are becoming literal walking revival. They are truly ambassadors, sent ones, representatives, of the God of fiery passion on the earth. They can be mocked, ridiculed, even killed, but they cannot be stopped.

When the gospel of the kingdom began to affect Thessalonica, some jealous, threatened, wicked people in the city created a mob scene and cried out in an attempt to stop revival:

> "These men who have *turned the world upside down* have come here also, and Jason has received them into his house and privately protected them! And they are all ignoring and acting contrary to the decrees of Caesar, [actually] asserting that there is another king, one Jesus!"
>
> --Acts 17:6, AMP

This is the *normal* affect believers who are walking in revival have on a city. Demons are angry, evil people are threatened, religious leaders are jealous, right alongside of people who are being saved, healed, and delivered. In short, nothing can stay the same!

Notice that the proclamation of these revivalists has nothing to do with planting a church or gathering people. It is a kingdom revolution centered around another king, "one Jesus!" This is what is so upsetting to the world and the enemy! The early church never allowed the smoke of programs or church structure to distract them from focusing on exalting the King and on building the kingdom. They were relentlessly "kingdom" in their orientation.

In kingdom churches, revival is our default setting, and the church is made up of revivalists. Therefore, instead of building program-based design (PBD) churches, we build *revival-based design* (RBD) churches. Revival-based design churches expect things to change. They expect miracles to happen. They expect people to come to Christ. They count on the spontaneous expansion of the church, and they position themselves accordingly. Stronger nets. Simple, flexible wineskins. Rapid reproduction of disciples. The church unleashed to baptize on the spot. A way for spontaneous Bible studies to spring up as needed and in the neighborhoods where people are getting saved. A type of church that is free from bureaucracy and red tape so it can rapidly respond to and agree with all God is doing.

In the West, we have often planned our programs and church structures without any real notion that God could save over 3,000 in a day as He did in Acts 2. Because there is a lack of expectation and a lack of urgency, we have often *counted on* taking 20-30 years to "raise up" and release an elder. In many of our churches, we sadly create a system of mistrust, where a new person, regardless of their maturity in Christ, is required to sit around for six months while we look them over and figure out if we trust them enough to work in children's ministry or to hand out bulletins.

In the early church, leaders were reproduced much more quickly. Jesus turned young business leaders into powerful apostles in less than four years. Throughout the Scriptures, God seems to entrust individuals with ministry responsibilities far more quickly than we do in the church of the West. Jeremiah the prophet was released somewhere in his teenage years. He wasn't a "junior" prophet, but a Prophet to nations! Josiah was one of the most radical kings in the history of Israel. He became king when he was eight years old! God foresaw this and approved it, prophesying about Josiah by name, so at 16, when Josiah read the law and saw his name mentioned, he became "walking revival" from that point forward. He removed the high places, which no other king had done.

Intensity Is Accessible

What about you? Can you live with kingdom intensity as a student, a mom, a contractor? Yes! Kingdom intensity is available to the person with a seemingly "normal" life.

While you may feel that your external circumstances are unimpressive, God looks upon the heart. Your "normal" exterior vocation doesn't need to define your "revivalist" interior life! He sees your extravagant devotion and the strong desire for Him that's inside of you while you sell jewelry or make dinners or attend classes or show up faithfully at your job. Kingdom intensity is for everyone!

> "Whatever your hand finds to do, do it with all your might...heartily, as for the Lord rather than for men."
> --Eccl. 9:10; Col. 3:23

This is sustainable intensity, burning by the Spirit of God in the human spirit, regardless of circumstances, geography or any other factor that may have limited our thinking in the past.

Running With Joy

People rooted in God's love can live with kingdom intensity. It works. One of my favorite verses in the Bible is 1 Chronicles 16:10 (repeated in Psalm 105:3)--

"Let the hearts of those who seek the Lord be glad."

This verse has meant so much to me as I am growing into an intense lover of God and an ardent pursuer of His kingdom. *There is joy in the seeking and joy in the finding.* It is not simply those who attain a new level in God or those who have radical, memorable experiences (although we want these things!) who have joy. Great joy is available on the journey! As we pursue Him, we find joy *along the way.* This is a strong comfort and encouragement to all of us. It guards us from elitism and hyperspirituality. We are glad in the seeking!

Like children, we find pleasure in the "hide and seek" reality of God. We are not put off by our pursuit of Him.

We are not intense in a sad way. Rather than being miserable, we are joyful in our childlike pursuit of God! We find Him compelling, and we pursue Him and His kingdom with childlike wonder and abandonment.

Comparison is a trap, and appearances can be deceiving! Who was more intense in the Scriptures: Peter, who loudly proclaimed he wouldn't deny the Lord (and then did anyway), or Anna, who spent her time in secret, praying and fasting night and day in the temple (cf. Luke 2:36)? Who is more intense, the preacher shouting powerful prose, or the dad, weeping quietly over his sleeping children, asking God to cover and protect them? Kingdom intensity is sustainable, because it works in real life, with real people, who are focused on Jesus in simple devotion to Him.

Running To Win

In order to build kingdom churches with Biblical intensity, our pace of thinking and activity as a corporate people will need to change. Revivalists are people who run! Their pace is more vigorous than what we're used to in the West, and in order to build kingdom churches together, our default pace will need to change!

There are several ways to relate to God in terms of our activity. The Bible speaks of certain postures we can and should have before God, either expressed in our physical conduct or metaphorically in our spiritual walk with Him.

> **Lying Down.** In Psalm 23:2, David describes one desirable posture before God: "He makes me *lie down* in green pastures." Laying or lying down speaks of a posture of dependency, rest, refueling, death to self, and surrender to God as living sacrifices. It is good for individuals and churches to lie down before the Lord. Over the past decade or so, many churches have discovered the posture of lying down for the sake of renewal, refreshing, and rest in the Father's love.

> **Bowing Down/Kneeling.** David also models a posture of bowing down and kneeling in Psalm 95:6 when he says, "Come let us *bow down* in worship; let us *kneel* before the LORD our Maker." This posture represents a heart of humility and reverent worship before Almighty God. The saints of old understood the importance of kneeling and bowing low, and God is helping the church in the West embrace a widespread kneeling and bowing low before Him. This is good!

Sitting. The first two chapters of Ephesians, which describe our position in Christ, tell us that Jesus is seated at the right hand of the Father (1:20), and that we are seated with Him in the heavenly realms (2:6). Sitting has to do with sonship and strength of position. It is a position of honor and privilege given to us by the Father. In the place of sitting, we can enjoy relationship with God as His heirs. We are sitting at His table, feasting on His provision for us, and we are sitting in heaven, enjoying His perspective. How the church needs to sit with God!

Standing. Standing is our posture of strength, endurance, and victory. Standing speaks of stability. It is our unwillingness to be moved by circumstances, difficulties, and even demonic attack. Ephesians 6 tells us to take our stand against the devil's schemes, so that when difficult times come, we may be able to stand our ground, and after we have done everything, we find ourselves still standing. We are commanded to stand firm while wearing the full armor of God.

Walking. Galatians 5 tells every believer to walk in the Spirit. We are told to avoid walking in the pathway of wicked people (Ps. 1), but instead to walk with like-minded people (Amos 3:3). Walking is a metaphor for flow and continuity of life. It speaks of our maturity and the consistency of our lifestyle as expressed in our actions. We walk in the light and love of God while following in the footsteps of Jesus Christ (1 Jn. 1:7; 2 Jn. 1:6; 1 Jn.2:6).

Running. If we take the time to *lie down* with the Lord, to *bow low and kneel* before Him, to *stand* up and fight, to *walk* with God and our brothers and sisters, then it is only appropriate that we would finally get to RUN! It is time for the church in the West to run. In fact, it is the promise of God that as we engage in these other postures, we will run...and not grow weary! (cf. Isa. 40:29-31) Running has to do with acceleration, multiplication, and miracles. It is the kind of life that cannot be fully explained. It is a holy urgency and a joyful aggressiveness that removes self-consciousness and faulty inhibitions. When Mary found out that Jesus had risen from the grave, she ran to tell the disciples, and when Peter and John heard, they ran back to the tomb! Running is part of the Christian experience, and it is a vital expression of kingdom intensity. Churches in the West are going to learn how to run together!

Recently our local church started a Running Club. Because we live near the beach, a group of us meet several afternoons each week to run together. The running club is for exercise, but more importantly, it is a metaphor for what God is doing with us spiritually. We are learning how to run together. What we find is that everyone runs at a different pace. Some are not in the right condition to run, so they walk all or part of the way. But no one is criticized for where they're at. Instead, we all encourage each other. We pray and then start together at the same time. Those who finish first wait for the rest and cheer them on as the cross the finish line.

In kingdom churches, it is not good enough if the pastor and staff get to fulfill their destiny while everyone else watches and applauds. It is time for every believer in every church in the West to reach their full potential and to fulfill their destiny in Christ. We are living in a divine season of acceleration, and we are learning how to run together. There is joy in running, but there is more joy in running together. Kingdom churches are designed so everyone can run. For that to happen, we must learn how to become a kingdom of priests. We'll look at that subject in our next chapter.

Chapter Four
Kingdom PRIESTS

"....He has made us to be a kingdom, priests to His God
and Father..." --Rev. 1:6

The dream that has been growing in the heart of many
people in the Western church has a lot to do with the now
common Christian phrase, *the priesthood of all believers.*
More and more people are dreaming of communities of faith
where the playing field has been leveled and where everyone
gets to play. There is a yearning in every believer to be in the
company of other believers who embody mutual respect,
who give honor where honor is due, who truly rejoice to see
everyone reach his or her full potential in Christ, and where
there is a refreshing absence of hierarchical dominance and
control. Many of us have carried on an internal discussion,
wondering if in fact this could be God's very will, however
seemingly idealistic, while knowing deep down that it
absolutely must be so; and wondering how in the world this
dynamic reality could ever happen in the kinds of churches
we have been producing, while also hoping beyond hope
that we could be a part of something so joyously and
refreshingly Biblical as this functional priesthood.

We are on the verge of seeing widespread fulfillment of
the functioning reality of the priesthood of every believer.
This generation will have the privilege of walking in
something that many previous generations have longed for
but not really touched. We are becoming what we were
made to be all along: kingdom priests.

THE PROMISE OF PRIESTHOOD

I am thrilled beyond description to be part of a generation that will make our Father's heart glad (Prov. 10:1) by becoming what He has intended for us to become. Aren't you? Out of all the generations that have gone before us, we are a generation that is going to live out the revelation of the priesthood! The hope that every believer could serve God on equal footing with every other believer didn't originate with this generation. Even Martin Luther, great reformationist that he was, didn't invent this reality. The promise of a functional priesthood of every believer goes farther back, mentioned several times in the New Testament but originating thousands of years ago in the book of Exodus. Think about that for a minute. God has been waiting for a long, long time to see all of His people on earth live like priests at the same time! We are entering into a kairos moment.

Old Testament Priests

In one of the more tender passages in the Old Testament, God speaks of the longing in His own heart:

> "Then Moses went up to God, and the LORD called to him from the mountain and said, 'This is what you are to say to the house of Jacob and what you are to tell the people of Israel: "You yourselves have seen what I did to Egypt, and how I carried you on eagles' wings and brought you to myself. Now if you obey me fully and keep my covenant, then out of all the nations you will be my treasured possession. Although the whole earth is mine, *you will be for me a kingdom of priests* and a holy nation." These are the words you are to speak to the Israelites."'" --Ex. 19:3-6

We only know God as He reveals Himself, and this exchange is one of those places in Scripture where there is an intimate revelation into God's heart and thought process. The great I

AM initiates a conversation where He reveals vulnerability in His own heart by vocalizing what He deeply desires. He describes the strength of love He has for His people by narrating His version of their recent history coming out of Egypt. God discloses that it wasn't simply the great and powerful Almighty dramatically delivering a people out of a pagan nation so that someday these stories would be recounted in church classes all across the world. Instead, He remembers it as a time when He carried His people "on eagles' wings"--not to a desert, nor even to a promised land, but to Himself. While the subject of this chapter on priesthood is not primarily the profound love of God, we could pitch our tents here for quite some time and worship before a God like this. He is worthy of our praise. O blessed be the name of God most high! His love endures forever. We are His treasured possession! Thank You, most beautiful God, for loving us the way that You do.

After speaking tenderly to His people, the LORD then offers a profound invitation in vv. 5-6. Even though, He says, the whole earth is mine, and I have everything under my control and Lordship, I will gladly disperse priestly hearts and roles among all my people so every single one of you can partner with me in ministry. God is saying, in effect, that the Aaronic priesthood system He is about to set up is really only a picture of what His heart desires for all His people. While a few would be designated to serve in an official, paid, full-time capacity in the tabernacle, God's real desire is that all of His people would love and serve Him as priests, regardless of their vocational role in society.

"you will be for me a kingdom of priests..."

Within this Old Covenant context, specific priestly activities belonged to the priests and Levites. Priests were male descendants of Aaron, who was a Levite (Numbers 3:10), and Levites were other male members of the tribe of Levi. The primary duties of the priesthood took place in the tabernacle and later in the temple. Priests looked after the vessels used during special ceremonies and performed the offerings and sacrifices. The Levites assisted the priests and served the congregation in the temple. They sang the psalms, carried out administrative functions, such as keeping the temple courts clean and helping to prepare certain sacrifices and offerings, and they also had a teaching function. What was meant to occur in every believer's home occurred in a larger and more ceremonial way in the temple, and what occurred in the temple was a spiritual picture of the kinds of activities God had reserved for all of His people, a kingdom of priests.

New Testament Priests

The priesthood was always about the kingdom, even under the Old Covenant. Priesthood has never been about the church. God's intention is that these priests would be authorized through His kingdom rather than through a papal system of human government. God initiated priests of the kingdom, and collectively, a kingdom of priests. When we come to the New Testament, we see that under the New Covenant, our interactions with the temple and thus the ceremonial law of the Old Covenant ceased from operation and relevance. Nevertheless, God persists in sharing His dream with His people again under the New Covenant, first through Peter and then through John:

> "As you come to him, the living Stone--rejected by men but chosen by God and precious to him--you also, like living stones, are being built into a spiritual house to be a *holy priesthood*, offering spiritual sacrifices acceptable to God through Jesus Christ. For...you are a chosen people, a *royal priesthood*, a holy nation, a people belonging to God, that you may declare the praises of him who called you out of darkness into his wonderful light. Once you were not a people, but now you are the people of God; once you had not received mercy, but now you have received mercy." --1 Pet. 2:4-10

"[Jesus Christ] loves us and has freed us from our sins by his blood, and has made us to be a *kingdom and priests* to serve his God and Father..." --Rev. 1:5-6

"Then I saw a Lamb, looking as if it had been slain, standing in the center of the throne, encircled by the four living creatures and the elders...And they sang a new song: "You are worthy to take the scroll and to open its seals, because you were slain, and with your blood you purchased men for God from every tribe and language and people and nation. You have made them to be a *kingdom and priests* to serve our God, and *they will reign on the earth.*" --Rev. 5:6-10

"Blessed and holy are those who have part in the first resurrection. The second death has no power over them, but *they will be priests of God and of Christ and will reign with him for a thousand years.*" --Rev. 20:6

Peter says twice in a few verses that collectively we are a priesthood, both holy (set apart) and royal (privileged with access and authority). Our very identity as the people of God is synonymous with our role as a priesthood. The Apostle John elaborates by describing the priesthood as part of what Christ purchased for us on the cross. Notice that in the passages in Revelation, we have already been made into priests and we will also be priests in the era of the millennium.

In other words, our role as priests is permanent and significant. With the physical temple now long gone, these Scriptures urge us under the New Covenant to understand our privilege and responsibility before God and man.

Our ministry as priests under the New Covenant is comprised of two basic realities: ministering to the Person of God, and serving God by ministering to people. One of the tragedies of any believer or church, whether the church in Ephesus then or much of the church in the West today, is when we lose the art of ministering to the Person of God:

"Yet I hold this against you: You have forsaken your first love." --Rev. 2:4

The church in Ephesus was excellent at serving God, but they had neglected their primary priestly role of ministry to the Person of God. Ministry to God was a significant part of the role of the priests in the Old Testament, and it was modeled for us by the early church in Acts 13:

"While they were ministering to the Lord and fasting, the Holy Spirit said..." --Acts 13:2

As the early church focused on the Person of God, their first priestly ministry, God released apostolic strategy for their second priestly ministry of serving, in this case the sending of church planters.

Several years ago I received an exhortative word of prophecy touching on this very point. Among other things, this person said to me, *"Never let your zeal for serving Him get ahead of your prayer for seeking Him."* This was an exhortation from the Lord to me so I would remember my priestly ministries and give them the proper priority in my heart and life.

THE KINGDOM TENSION
OF INDIVIDUAL AND CORPORATE CHRISTIANITY

While it is true that each believer is a priest, it is also true that God intends for us to be built together as a priesthood. These two truths exist side by side in the Scriptures, creating a 'both/and' kingdom tension. Let's look at what is at stake.

The Powerful Dynamic Of Individual Christianity

One of the primary reasons for the dramatic increase in holy dissatisfaction is that for too long, the leadership of the church has been underemphasizing the powerful dynamic of individual Christianity. We who are leaders in the church have been guilty of disempowering the individual believer, and we really owe the church an apology. In its most innocuous form, there has been a surprising lack of Biblical understanding. However, we also need to acknowledge the elephant in the middle of the room. Church leadership has often used its positional authority to control believers who have expressed a desire for more individual freedom within the church. Because we haven't known what to do with individuals who are strong in their expression and who have a high view of their individual authority in Christ, we have overpreached corporate Christianity. We have continually emphasized the dimensions of Christianity that have to do with family, togetherness, belonging, and membership. Please don't misunderstand. These truths are vital and I believe in their validity, but when they are presented out of balance they can do great damage. And let's face it: they have been presented out of balance.

It is time to emphasize the individual realities of Christianity that will liberate a generation of believers to be and do the very thing we have tried to accomplish through church programs. Pastors, don't be afraid. The people you serve will appreciate you so much more if you will honor their individuality instead of being threatened by it. The people of God are starving to be affirmed for who they are and where they're at as individuals, regardless of their level of participation in church programs.

Part of the role of a *kingdom church* is to communicate high value for individual Christianity and to affirm the validity of contributions to the kingdom made by the people of God in whatever stage or sphere of life they find themselves. I am not only saying that people need to be encouraged to "be the church" in the marketplace, although that is true. Nor am I primarily saying that we must release people to serve in any ministry in the church that matches their gifting, although, again, that is probably a good thing to say to people. Actually, the things I am talking about have nothing to do with the corporate church. There are truths in the New

Testament that need to be meditated on before we immediately try to qualify them. Every believer has both the privilege and responsibility to stand before God as a priest without qualification. Here are a few truths that illustrate this fact:

We Are Complete In Christ. As an individual believer, without any input or help from anyone else in or out of the church, I am absolutely, 100% complete in Jesus Christ, because fullness and completeness have been given to me as a gift (Col. 2:9-10). I have already received everything I need to be successful in life and to be godly by His divine power (2 Pet. 1:3) which works mightily in me (Col. 1:29). Amazingly, I have been given every single spiritual blessing that exists from my Father, in the Person of Jesus Christ (Eph. 1:3). All of this should be obvious, of course, because Jesus died for me, but I am doubly assured that with Christ, I am freely given all things (Rom. 8:32). If, in a difficult moment, I forget how complete I am in Christ, all I have to do is remember how much my Father is for me, and He will make all grace abound towards me so that in all things, at all times, having all that I need, I will abound (2 Cor. 9:8). If there is any doubt about what I do or do not have, Paul says plainly that all things are mine (1 Cor. 3:21).

God Is Our Clergy. God is our Senior Pastor! Clergy as mediation is entirely unbiblical, because there is only One mediator, the man Christ Jesus (1 Tim. 2:5). God, in fact, is our Clergy, because we go to Him to confess our sins (1 Jn. 1:9), and even when we go to people to seek prayer, it is to 'one another', not just to a pastor (Jms. 5:16). The Father is our Source (1 Cor. 8:6), and when we look to people as our Source, we commit great sin (Jer. 2:13). God is our covering (Ps. 91:4) and His hand of blessing covers us in everything (Isa. 51:16). We already know the truth, because we have an anointing from God that is more important than any human teaching (1 Jn. 2:20, 27). If we lack any understanding, the Holy Spirit is our Teacher and Counselor and He will teach us all things (Jn. 14:26), not in words taught by human wisdom but in words taught by the Spirit (1 Cor. 2:14). Not only does Jesus provide us with the most wonderful counsel (Isa. 9:6), but Jesus Himself is our great Intercessor (Heb. 7:25), along with the Holy Spirit, who prays for us in our weakness (Rom. 8:26). In the Father, Son, and Holy Spirit, we have the best pastoral team there is! (2 Cor. 13:14).

Ministry Belongs To Every Believer. Because we are a kingdom of priests (Rev. 1:5), we have inherited a ministry straight from heaven (2 Cor. 5:18). We are all commissioned as ambassadors (2 Cor. 5:20) and authorized by Jesus Himself to make disciples (Mt. 28:19), which includes the activities of baptism, teaching, and modeling the Christian life (Mt. 28:19-20; 2 Tim. 2:2). We have each received a unique ministry destiny (Eph. 2:10) and unique gifts to administer God's grace (1 Pet. 4:10). We must obey God rather than men (Acts 5:29) because we will each be held individually accountable to God at judgment for our ministry effectiveness (1 Cor. 3:13). Therefore, we must be motivated by God Himself (2 Cor. 5:14) to fulfill our ministries that we have received from God Himself (Col. 4:17), because we are responsible to God to discharge all the duties of our ministry (2 Tim. 4:5). The responsibility of our actions in life and ministry falls on each individual believer (Gal. 6:4-5), as do our entrustments and individual rewards from God (Mt. 13:23; 25:15-28).

Now, when you read these truths, some questions may pop in your mind, like: "Then why do we need the church! And why do we need pastors?" That, my friend, is a healthy response to undiluted truth! It can startle us. It is the response Paul anticipated in Romans 5 when he spoke so freely about the grace of God that he anticipated the question: "Well, if grace is this good and free, why don't we just sin so grace will abound even more?" (Rom. 6:1). Grace is that amazing, and the priesthood of every believer is that amazing. The fact is, we must honor individual Christianity far more than we have been.

The Vital Necessity Of Corporate Christianity

The other truth that brings dynamic kingdom tension to the first is the vital necessity of corporate Christianity. (By corporate, I don't mean "of a corporation", but rather togetherness.) Regarding this issue of corporate Christianity, there is a powerful Biblical warning that needs to be trumpeted at this time, even as we're trumpeting the revolution into the priesthood of all believers and the strength of individual Christianity. With much freedom comes much responsibility. As more and more of the church is embracing holy dissatisfaction, there is a subtle deception occurring right alongside it. In 2 Thess. 2:7, Paul warns us about the mystery, or secret power, of lawlessness. The Greek word for lawlessness is "anomia", which means illegality. In other words, as the day draws near for Christ to return, there will be an increase in wicked, illegal operations in the world and in the church. In the church, there will be many who will no longer put up with sound, healthy doctrine (2 Tim. 4:3-4) even as it is preached and administrated through those with God-given authority (2 Tim. 4:1-2). These things will be occurring secretly or mysteriously in people's hearts and in murmurings. They will be difficult to detect, because they will not be talked about in the open but rather subtly administered through seemingly spiritual people! This is the definition of "musterion", or mystery. Even as we herald priests as individuals, we must also trumpet the priesthood as a group. Here are a few important realities regarding our corporate expression of Christianity:

We Are Called To Christian Relationships.
Through the book of 1 John and in many other places, we learn that our Christianity has to look like something--love in the context of relationship. The many "one another" Scriptures in the New Testament, which I won't take the space to enumerate here, clearly speak of the need for Christian relationship, for how can we fulfill a "one another" Scripture if we're not in relationship with other believers? It's not possible. We grow best in relationships, because it is in relationships that our character is formed. When I was a child, I had a poster on the wall of my bedroom with a photo of a rushing stream. The caption read: "Talent is produced in solitude, character in the stream of life." I heard of one mature prophet who had an experience where he was taken before the throne of God and asked one question: "Did you learn to love?" This reminds me of the children's movie, *Beauty And The Beast*, where Mrs. Potts says of the beast, "He's finally learned to love." Indeed, we need the mutual support and ministry of Christian relationships, and relationships provide a context for us to "learn to love." Love is our goal and aim in everything we're doing, and love happens in the context of relationships.

We Are Called To Dwell Together. More than simply knowing and relating to other Christian believers, we are called as Christians to actually dwell together in unity (Ps. 133). We are called living stones (1 Pet. 2:5), meant to be fitted together into a spiritual house, a corporate dwelling place of God in the Spirit (Eph. 2:22; Rev. 21:3). The early church modeled life together to such an extent that they were completely unified in their hearts and minds (Acts 4:32), and because they knew each others' lives and shared material possessions, there was no one needy among them (Acts 4:34). Part of this dwelling together means that we gather regularly (Heb. 10:25) just as the early church practiced (Acts 2:46; 5:12), for relationship and ministry (Acts 5:42). Each of us is called to bring our spiritual offering to the gathered assembly and to worship God together (1 Cor. 14:26). Every believer is designed by God to be part of something bigger than himself or herself and to be in an environment of mutual submission and accountability (Eph. 5:21).

We Are Called To Minister With Other Believers. While it is entirely true that we have been given a ministry by God, and while it is true that we must be responsible before God to fulfill our ministry, it is also true that we are called to join other Christians in service to God. Jesus modeled team ministry when he sent his disciples out two by two (Lk. 10:1). Moses learned the power of shared responsibility and team ministry from his father-in-law, Jethro (Ex. 18:13-26). Scripture teaches the power of working together by telling us that two are better than one (Eccl. 4:9-12) and that multiplication occurs when we work together. "Five of you will chase a hundred, and a hundred of you will chase ten thousand..." (Lev. 26:8). Paul clearly teaches us that we cannot walk in the completeness we are destined for unless we have all parts of the body functioning together (1 Cor. 12:12-27) and working together in the joints (i.e., places of coming together) of the body (Eph. 4:11-16). Ministry with other believers is part and parcel of what it means to be the church.

These two truths, individual and corporate Christianity, when honored and not diluted, create a powerful kingdom tension.

What are we to do with this tension? Clearly, the Scriptures teach both realities, and yet the struggle we've had over the years is how to reconcile the two dynamics in the local church setting. As we come together in corporate Christianity, how can we honor the individual? And, as individual believers, how can we come together in a way that results in Biblical expressions of church life? This kingdom tension is perhaps the premiere issue facing churches at this time. And in particular, over the past few decades, we have seen various ways that local churches have dealt with this dynamic kingdom tension.

FIVE KINDS OF CHURCHES

The priesthood of all believers is ultimately just a concept until we begin to look at how it works (or doesn't work) in the real setting of a body of believers. To move from concept to practice, let's take a look at the five most common ways that individual and corporate Christianity relate and interact in the context of a local church. Keep in mind that these assessments are not addressing all aspects of what is good or not so good in each type of church. We are simply addressing the issue of how the individual and the corporate dimensions of Christianity interact with each other in the context of a local church. Each of these five kinds of churches stand alone in their explanation, but as you read these descriptions, you may find that you or someone you know has actually progressed through each of these kinds of churches in sequence!

ONE: The Institutional Church

The institutional church is best characterized by its ongoing focus on *the church*. In other words, the goal of the church is the church. Now, *every* Christian church would claim that their focus is Jesus. We concede that in every Christian church the focus is Jesus! But what we're talking about specifically is how the local church relates to the individual. In the institutional church, the church is first and the individual is second. This means that the individual exists to serve the church, and the individual's validation comes through their participation in the church.

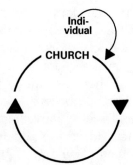

Who are the most important people in the institutional church? Those who are most engaged in the church's ministries and programs.

The good news about the institutional church is that many people who are part of institutional churches feel a part of something bigger than themselves. In the institutional church, people learn how to set aside their personal wishes for the greater good of the church, and since all of us need to learn to serve, the institutional church is a great environment to learn how to serve.

The difficulty with the institutional church is that people feel they are valued in the context of how they serve the institution. They begin to feel used and even resentful. After some years in the institutional church, many good, godly Christian people become either hurt, offended, or burned out, and they leave. They often don't feel their individuality is valued. Regardless of the reasons, Christians are leaving the institutional church by droves.

TWO: The Invitational Church

In the invitational church, the focus is on *growth*. The goal of the church is to reach out and gather people into the church. Therefore, the church is designed as a consumer-oriented place that takes special care to make sure the red carpet is rolled out for visitors and guests. A highly trained

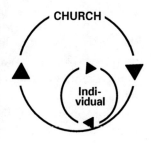

staff puts forth great effort to ensure the very best experience for everyone who comes to the church, with special attention paid to visitors. Invitational churches are often successful at growth because this is a large part of their goal and focus.

There are many wonderful aspects of the invitational church. I believe God sovereignly birthed the church growth and seeker movements to help the institutional church get beyond itself and start caring about the millions of people trying to find God but unable to fit into the institutional church. I deeply appreciate and value invitational churches, because they have come up with a way to re-create a modern day "Court Of The Gentiles" aspect of the temple, a place where God-seekers can come and find God. They have unselfishly set aside their desire for church to be about themselves, and they have designed church services for lost people and seekers. What a refreshing change when invitational churches hit the scene! They have really harvested many people for Jesus and helped thousands of churches become outward-focused. This is a good thing!

The difficulty with the invitational church is that the individual is essentially irrelevant. What I mean is, when most people walk into an invitational church, it really doesn't matter whether or not they show up. Why is this true? Because the invitational church has, by default, set the bar very low to make sure that whosoever will may come. However, the inadvertent message is that the individual is not really needed. Little is asked or required of people, and it is very clear that if they aren't part of the overall goal to facilitate growth, their gifts may not be needed. To prove the point: where do many of the people who have left institutional churches go? They often sit in the back of invitational churches where they can go unnoticed and where they can have very little asked of them. The invitational church is a great place to recover from the institutional church, and some go on and become involved in meaningful ways.

But often over time, two negative things happen to believers who have been in invitational churches. One, they become sedentary, consumer-oriented Christians. Those who joined the institutional church and who wanted to make a difference have all but lost their initial fire. Often they no longer burn with zeal for God and His purposes. Instead, they unwittingly adopt the culture of the invitational church into their Christianity, and they, too, lower the bar to the point where, for all intents and purposes, they are now just showing up at a weekend service. Or two, they begin to feel the need for a more personal, relational church, and they move on to something more personal and meaningful to them.

THREE: The Interpersonal Church

The interpersonal church is a refreshing change for many who spent years in the institutional and invitational church environments. The interpersonal church is best characterized by its focus on the *warmth and belonging of each individual.* Interpersonal churches 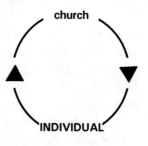 tend to be smaller in size, often meeting in homes or other more intimate settings. Interpersonal churches tend to be filled with people who either have left other church environments feeling unsatisfied or who chafe against church structure in general. As a result, these churches also tend to lower the bar, but in a different way. There is often more participation but in a very low-key, relaxed manner so as not to scare off or stress out people who are burned out on most aspects of familiar church life. Structure is simple and demands are few.

The interpersonal church is a refreshing alternative to both the institutional church and the invitational church. Of the three, it is the type of church that demonstrates value for each individual more readily and successfully. People who join interpersonal churches feel validated for who they are, and because the goal is the warmth and belonging of each individual, there is an atmosphere of acceptance. We've needed the influence of the interpersonal church to move us away from the CEO mentality of many churches. The interpersonal church is leading the way in creating environments of grace and acceptance.

The great strength of the interpersonal church is also its weakness. It is, by necessity, inward. If it becomes too outward or too large too quickly, the very warmth and belonging that made it special is lost, and the feelings of institutionalism rapidly increase, bringing uncomfortability for those who signed up for its smallness, simplicity, and closeness. Further, the interpersonal church has difficulty embracing individuals with strong gifting or authority from God. It is, by nature, very egalitarian. What does the interpersonal church do when Billy Graham shows up? He must go outside the church to preach, because the little group would be dominated by his legitimate gift from God. And, once Billy starts having impact, he will bring so many people with all kinds of personalities and expectations that he will mess up the environment! Many of these kinds of churches have great difficulty knowing what to do with someone who has a gift meant for a larger environment. Interpersonal churches can sometimes 'dumb down' the environment to such a basic level that people who feel unchallenged or who want to be more outward leave to find another place. If the interpersonal church ends up being a part of something bigger than itself, it thrives. But by itself, it remains incomplete and can leave mature, gifted saints feeling unsatisfied.

FOUR: The Individual Church

The very latest trend in church life is the individual church. The individual church is focused on *freedom* and obtains it to its maximum degree. Some of those who opt out of other types of churches do so because they are looking for the ultimate

expression of their individual Christianity. Individuals (and sometimes small families) who consider themselves the church all by themselves know what it is like to have no rules. And this is not entirely a bad thing.

There are some good reasons why the individual church is flourishing at this time in history. Many people are getting in touch with the fact that they are priests before the Lord and they are choosing to validate their individual Christianity by removing themselves from structures that often constrict or at least fail to affirm their individual Christian expression. They are weary of systems that put too much emphasis on leadership, submission, etc., and they are exploring another way to experience God. Those who have opted out of all forms of organized church life are a voice for change, and we would do well to listen to the Lord in the midst of this trend.

Of course, there is a down side. Individuals who do not participate in a community of believers are missing a huge part of the way Christianity was meant to be experienced. In their desire to walk in freedom as an individual, they are violating Scriptural principles and commands to dwell in community with and submission to other believers. Eventually, if they stay away from a community of faith, their own expression of faith will become lopsided, and they will be susceptible to the mystery of lawlessness. This temptation is not new. Hebrews 10:25 tells us not to forsake believer's gatherings, *"as is the habit of some."*

Nevertheless, the departure of individual believers from organized church must at least be sympathized with and understood. They are protesting the lack of viable options.

FIVE: The Interdependent Church

As we begin looking at the interdependent church, let me affirm again that each of the previous four kinds of church are providing at least some benefit. Although they each have faults and deficiencies, they are still serving the Lord and His people, and many of them will be around for years to come.

Whenever God adds something new to His work on the earth, His previous works still stand on their own merit. As long as there is mutual appreciation and understanding, all of these kinds of churches can get along and enjoy the contribution each one makes to the kingdom.

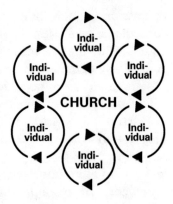

Having said that, my favorite kind of church from a Biblical and practical standpoint, as it relates to the kingdom tension between individual and corporate Christianity, is the *interdependent* church. The interdependent church focuses on *kingdom partnerships*. It is a relationally-based, network style structure rather than a hierarchy. It has similarities to each of the other four kinds of churches, but the contrasts are significant. Let's take a quick look at each one.

Like the institutional church, everyone in the interdependent church is involved in something bigger than themselves, but unlike the institutional church, there is no institution. It is a partnership of priests who have joined together as like-minded believers going after the same vision. There is no "church" to build, because the people are the church. Individual believers living for Christ in real life contexts is the goal of the interdependent church. Gatherings are really only to celebrate this fact and support one another in the process.

Like the invitational church, the interdependent church is an outward, missional church where everyone is meant to reach lost people. But unlike the invitational church, the default setting for outreach is not a "come ye" focus on numerous "services" as the primary net, but instead on a "go ye" mobilized army. Because each person is vital to the success of the whole, the interdependent church ultimately cannot move forward with just a great staff. The church fundamentally changes when each person walks into the room (and into the community of believers), because each person brings their own set of gifts and callings from God. It also means that a program-based design church cannot work where there is true interdependence, because ministries are largely determined by who shows up rather than simply by the declarations of the senior leader or board.

Like the interpersonal church, each person in the interdependent church is highly valued and appreciated. And like the interpersonal church, the interdependent church has no agenda for individuals, other than to help see each individual reach his or her full potential in Christ. But the interdependent church differs in that it is captivated by huge vision. Because of its commitment to fullness, the interdependent church could never be satisfied with an inward orientation. It is too missional for that. The interdependent church is vitally linked to other churches and ministries in the city/region. The interdependent church makes room for both smaller expressions of church life (i.e., cells, house churches, etc.) and larger gatherings (celebrations, multi-church gatherings, healing rooms, houses of prayer, conferences). Neither is seen as inferior, because both are Biblical, and both contexts reach the lost and help people fulfill their destinies in Christ.

And like the individual church, each person in the interdependent church is encouraged to fulfill their destiny in an environment of freedom. But unlike the individual church, the interdependent church honors the corporate Biblical mandate to dwell together and to submit to one another out of reverence for Christ.

The interdependent church means that each person is vital but not controlled; individuals are honored and respected; and the church is unleashed, without walls and rules to hold it back. While this paradigm of interdependence may at first glance appear unrealistic or even anarchistic to some, it is quite the opposite. Proverbs 29:18 tells us that it is the absence of vision, not control, that causes people to act in unrestrained ways. A holy vision for a kingdom of priests functioning together in mutual honor, mutual submission and interdependency is the God-given dream inside the hearts of

God's people! Given the opportunity to honor that dream, the church will model kingdom living in a fresh way, and we will all be pleasantly surprised with the outcome.

CHURCH WITHOUT WALLS

The goal here is the church unleashed, the church without walls, flowing in grace, giving room for one another, serving and laying down our lives individually and together, each person fulfilling his or her unique, God-given destiny while partnering with others to do the same.

The Mobilized Priesthood

Each person who is part of the interdependent church is living as a priest before God, in their world, and with the church. As priests before God, our first ministry is to Him, to both worship Him and to enjoy Him. As John Piper says, "God is most glorified in us when we are most satisfied in Him." We receive directly from God all that we need pertaining to life and godliness. We consecrate ourselves to Him unto a holy life, and then we press in for more of His Person, His Presence, His Power, His Provision, and His Peace in our lives! This is how the priests were to bless the people in Numbers 6:24-26, and this is how we are to receive blessing from God directly. He wants to bless us directly through the mediation of Christ. Individuals are directed to God as their Source.

Then, we function as priests in our world. This includes our home, our work environment, and everywhere we go. We become "walking revival" wherever we are, a literal mobile church, an open heaven, carriers of the glory of God to the streets. We are the priests, each one of us, of Joel 2, weeping and contending for souls between the porch (representative of God seekers) and the altar (representative of intimacy). We are priests of intimacy unto fruitfulness. In kingdom churches, this identity must be affirmed over and over until people get it and live it.

Finally, we can function as priests in the contexts of Christian friendships that we call "church." The church is about life-giving relationships rather than gatherings. When we gather, we don't primarily assemble in the style of the synagogue: to learn, to receive, to evaluate, and to contemplate, but rather we assemble in the style of the temple: to worship, to pray, to encounter God, and to bring our offering. We come as living stones, fitted together in the house of God as a corporate dwelling place.

Priestly 'Order'

Even though we've meant well, I believe that for years we've been miscommunicating wrong priorities in the church. As I was being trained in church environments to pastor, I was taught that you could essentially map out a view of the church in concentric circles. The outermost circle represented the people who weren't a part of the church but were coming your way--the seekers. The next circle represented the people of the church who were members--

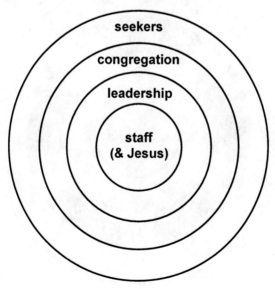

the congregation. The next circle represented the people who were serving and leading in the church--leadership. The final circle represented the inner circle of the pastoral staff. Over the years I have seen variations, but this is a commonly held view of the church. On the previous page is a diagram of this view of the church and how people relate to it.

Now, there are a couple of unintentional but nevertheless important miscommunications in this diagram and perhaps in the thinking behind it. First, it implies that in order to get closer to Jesus, you have to become more committed to the church, because the most spiritual people are in the center. Second, it views the life of the individual in relationship to the church and therefore creates an artificial mediation process and unintended institutionalism. I do not believe the Biblical goal of the church is to move people toward the center of these kinds of circles, because I believe the New Testament would diagram things completely differently.

Here is what I think is a more Biblically accurate diagram. For clarity's sake, I have left out some details in this diagram, but I want to point out a few important truths about this

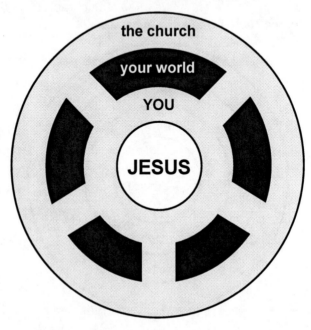

paradigm. First, only Jesus is in the center. No pastor, staff, or church should ever be there. Second, you and I as individuals are closest to Jesus. This honors individual Christianity without mediation and communicates both the privilege and responsibility of each believer to seek the Lord for all we need. Third, your world is next, which honors you as a priest bringing revival to your world. It speaks of the ministry that you have in your oikos (sphere of influence) without any red tape or church bureaucracy. And finally, the church is outside of it all, with the spokes representing your connection to the church. These spokes represent ministry to you and your family to strengthen and equip you as a priest, and they represent your partnership in servanthood ministry in team with others that becomes a context for you to equip and empower those in your God-given ministry sphere.

Let's Repent!

God brings about repentance by changing our minds. Once we see things from his perspective, we can easily change our behavior, because we believe in the changes we are making. We are learning to see the church and ourselves differently, and from that place of a paradigm shift, we can begin to see how these things translate into shifts in our activities within the church. We are learning to become the church without walls or ceiling! Repentance means our mind catches up with what God is already doing in our hearts. We agree with Him by changing directions and allow Him to realign our thought patterns so we are consistent and not in turmoil.

In order to really live as a church without walls, it is essential that we gain new understanding of the role of leadership. As the church is becoming empowered, unleashed, and mobilized, what do we do with leaders? [Do we even need them? :-)] In the next two chapters, we'll be tackling the rather large subject of authority and leadership in kingdom churches.

Chapter Five
Kingdom AUTHORITY

"Then I heard a loud voice in heaven say: 'Now have come the salvation and the power and the *kingdom* of our God, and the *authority* of his Christ...' " --Rev. 12:10

For us to function as kingdom priests who build kingdom churches, it is essential that we understand and walk in God's authority. The two are linked. The *kingdom* of God is advanced through the *authority* of Christ. Jesus explained this principle of kingdom authority in the Great Commission:

"All *authority* in heaven and on earth has been given to me. *Therefore go* and *make disciples* of all nations, *baptizing* them in the name of the Father and of the Son and of the Holy Spirit, and *teaching* them to obey everything I have commanded you..." --Mt. 28:18-20

The kingdom activities mentioned in the Great Commission of going to the nations, making disciples, baptizing, and teaching are directly linked to the complete authority of Jesus that has been extended to us. As kingdom priests, we have been authorized and credentialed by God to advance His kingdom. And yet, even though we have everything we need available to us, we often find believers in the West lacking effectiveness in advancing the kingdom. Therefore, we want to see kingdom churches that are full of kingdom priests functioning in kingdom authority.

TYPES OF AUTHORITY

There are four types of authority revealed in the Scriptures that are vital to building kingdom churches. They are: (1) *positional* authority (i.e., the authority of the believer); (2) *spiritual* authority; (3) *relational* authority; and (4) *delegated* authority. Positional and spiritual authority originate from God alone and are released directly to and through each individual believer, regardless of human relationships. Relational and delegated authority function only in the context of human relationships and spheres of influence. They are dependent on right relationships.

Each of these four kinds of authority serve a unique purpose and must be functioning in the local church. When exercised rightly and used in proper proportion, they unlock the church to move forward and to function in kingdom rhythm.

Positional Authority (The Authority Of The Believer)

Because we belong to Christ and are indwelt by the Holy Spirit, every believer carries internal, resident authority. At one time, before coming to Christ, we were people without identity and place (1 Pet. 2:10). Now, having been adopted into God's family as His own dear children (1 Jn. 3:1), we have become royalty! (1 Pet. 2:9). As His children, we are His heirs (Rom. 8:17) and carry a unique place of privilege and position.

Whatever we need to do, He provides the power and wisdom we need to get it done (1 Cor. 1:24). Wherever we need to go, He goes with us, because we are His representatives (2 Cor. 5:20). When we invoke the Name of Jesus in prayer according to God's will, results happen! Our prayers are answered as though Jesus prayed, and the enemy is defeated (Jn. 14:14; Rev. 12:11).

The significant authority that God gives to each believer is our *primary* type of authority and ought to be the type of authority in the church that is most encouraged and exercised. This type of authority empowers the priesthood of every believer. It is equally accessible by every Christian. It is what we need in order to accomplish the clear commands of Scripture. When every believer in the church understands and walks in this authority, there is great joy and freedom in the body. *To build kingdom churches, we must focus our equipping and empowering efforts on the authority that each believer has been afforded in Christ.*

Spiritual Authority

While every believer walks equally in the bestowed, positional authority gained through our relationship with the Person of Christ, some believers walk in and carry a more significant *spiritual* authority than others. All of God's authority is ultimately spiritual, but spiritual authority refers to a dynamic reality operating through believers in various degrees that comes from their place of intimacy with God, history with God, sovereign choice, and the resulting graces released by God. This authority is experiential and at times might also be called anointing. It is not dependent on a position in the church, because it comes straight from heaven. It gives force and credibility to those who walk in it, and it separates those who carry authentic weightiness in God from those who simply insist on authority because of their title or structural position. We notice it, for example, when we gravitate to certain people when asking for prayer. We know that they walk in something that will strengthen our heart. We know that their prayers will be answered. We know that they have significant spiritual authority. They *really walk* in the authority of the believer!

When Jesus spoke, the crowds marveled at the spiritual authority they could tangibly feel accompanying his words (Matt. 7:28-29). It had nothing to do with his position as a spiritual teacher or rabbi in Israel, because there were many religious leaders teaching the people. Jesus stood out because a tangible authority went out with His words. When

Peter and John stood boldly before the priests and the Sadducees and proclaimed the gospel, the religious leaders "took note" that these men had been with Jesus (Acts 4:13). The Greek word for "took note" is epiginosko, a compound word meaning to really know through experience. It was tangibly evident that these men carried an authority the religious leaders could not refute. Paul the apostle repeatedly claimed he had received spiritual authority directly from the Lord (2 Cor. 13:10; 1 Tim. 4:2). This heaven-sent authority was related to Paul's ministry function and not simply his role as a believer who was part of God's family. It was not released through elders or any other church leadership. It was spiritual authority.

Relational Authority

Relational authority is the grace and permission given from one believer to another to speak into and minister, founded in trust and respect. We speak of "history" with someone, and we know that they have a proven track record with which we can feel safe. This relational authority is developed over time as we serve one another and care for one another in love.

Someone said, "People don't care how much you know until they know how much you care." This kind of statement reflects the reality of relational authority. When I know that you care about me, and when there is enough of a relational connection between us, I can more freely share my heart and invite you to speak into my life. This is authority that I give to you because I trust you.

The Apostle Paul walked in all four types of authority during his ministry. His relationship with the Corinthian church illustrates the multiple types of authority he exercised in the church. In addition to the *positional* authority he had as a believer in Jesus Christ, Paul also had great *spiritual* authority from God with the Corinthians (2 Cor. 10:8; 13:10). He was also commissioned on his missionary journeys through the *delegated* authority of the church in Antioch and

Jerusalem. But even though all this was true, and even though he was an apostle, Paul often appealed simply to the relational love that he shared with the Corinthians that released appropriate *relational* authority:

> "We have spoken freely to you, Corinthians, and opened wide our hearts also. We are not withholding our affection from you, but you are withholding yours from us. As a fair exchange--I speak as to my children--open wide your hearts also." --2 Cor. 6:11-13

Delegated Authority

Authority given by God to individuals that is then released from person to person is called delegated authority. Scripture recognizes that all delegated authority originates with God, regardless of whether or not people use delegated authority in a right way. In Rom. 13:1 and 1 Pet. 2:13, this delegated authority is called "governing" or "institutional" authority, because it relates to government, law enforcement, and the court system. To rebel against this delegated authority is to rebel against God (Rom. 13:2). We are called to submit to such authority for the Lord's sake (1 Pet. 2:13).

Delegated authority is also given in the church, although there are differing opinions on how much, to whom this authority is given, and what it includes. One thing is certain: delegated, structural authority has been grossly overemphasized in the church, and the authority of the believer, spiritual authority, and relational authority have all been underemphasized and underappreciated.

Authority In Proportion. How these types of authority are proportioned, exercised, and encouraged among believers is a key issue in kingdom churches. Let's think about a financial illustration. When discussing investments, many financial advisors use a pyramid to illustrate wise investing. They encourage investors to wisely distribute their investments by putting the largest sums of money in the most secure investments, represented by the largest portion of a triangle at the base. Slightly more risky investments, with a potentially higher yield, are represented by a smaller portion of the pyramid in a narrower, middle section of the triangle. And the smallest, top area of the triangle represents the riskiest but potentially very rewarding investments. Authority in the church works much the same way, as illustrated in the following triangles. [Note that in these diagrams, for simplicity of understanding, spiritual and relational authority are represented as one section to form 3 parts of the triangle.]

Fig. A on the following page represents the way we are meant to think about authority. The large foundation and base is the authority of the believer. This levels the playing field, deemphasizes position and title, keeps our Christianity based in faith rather than subjectivity, and makes the promises of God equally accessible to every believer. Just above that is relational authority that is cultivated both vertically, in a personal relationship with God, and horizontally, in relationship with people. It is the endorsement of our credibility by the Holy Spirit, who puts authority on our words and deeds. He "backs up our act." And finally, like those riskier but potentially rewarding investments, delegated authority in the church has a small, powerful role to play. Delegated authority released well can help the heart of individual believers to soar and reach their full potential in Christ. But handled poorly through overemphasis, delegated authority can cause difficulty and injury.

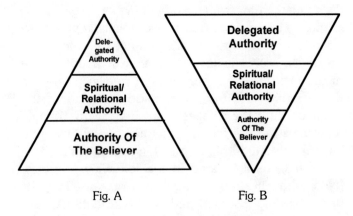

Fig. A   Fig. B

This is the problem with the upside down triangle in Fig. B. It overemphasizes delegated authority to the loss of the individual. Fig. B illustrates how the church in the West has typically handled authority. In North American churches, we have continually preached submission to delegated authority in the church, while failing to really honor the authority of the believer and recognize spiritual authority in people without a particular position in the church. [Note: Delegated authority as indicated in these triangles can be represented in the church by any governmental style: a senior pastor, a board, a congregation, a team/staff, etc.]

A Sensitive Matter. The subject of delegated authority has become a sensitive issue for many in the West and a painful topic of discussion. A large percentage of Western believers have stories to tell of how they have been abused, dominated, or "burned" by church leadership. In worse case scenarios, delegated authority has been like a giant club, beating people into submission, with a major overemphasis on the responsibility of the people to the institution of the church. Several books on the subject of spiritual abuse have been written over the past few decades in an attempt to bring balance and healing to an emotionally charged issue for many. Added to the mix is the large number of Christian leaders who have fallen into disrepute and who have broken trust with their followers.

This negative connotation surrounding authority is further reinforced through our culture. In America, scandals and misuse of power by those in positions of authority and positions of trust have become epidemic over the past few decades. From sports figures, to corporate CEOs, to White House personnel, to the military, we have seen so much abuse of positional authority that it is not surprising that a large percentage of Westerners have grown skeptical of most or all forms of human authority.

Of course, many church leaders have their own stories about how they have been undermined, manipulated, or verbally assaulted by church members! The bottom line is that delegated authority has become a dividing line in the church.

Unfortunately, the net result is that even the word "authority" as it relates to human beings now carries negative connotations for many in the church. A growing number of Christians believe authority is "bad." Sadly, many believers have come to "despise authority" (2 Pet. 2:10), even though authority is given by God to humanity as a gift for our good (Rom. 12:8; 13:1-2).

I once received a gentle rebuke from a godly saint who told me that, because of my past, I was perceiving authority as something bad instead of as a gift from God--and that I needed to repent! As I thought about his comment to me, I realized I had observed church leaders who had mishandled God's authority. Somewhere along the line I had made the unspoken, internal decision that because I didn't want to abuse authority the way I had seen it done, I would avoid using delegated authority. In my mind, it only

injured people. I had judged and condemned
something that God gave to the church as a gift.
Many Christians in North America have also made
this same unfortunate judgment.

What was meant to be a joyous New Testament
experience of exercising the authority of the King to
further His kingdom has instead become a confusing
and painful journey for far too many otherwise
sincere believers, both pastors and parishioners alike.
Understanding how authority works in kingdom
churches is key to building the kinds of churches that
empower rather than disable.

TYPES OF GOVERNMENT

Government is another one of those hot potatoes! Like the
word "authority" in churches, church government has few
avid supporters and a growing number of detractors. Typical
definitions of the word really don't help, either. In general,
government is (1) a group of people *who have the power* to
make and enforce laws; or (2) a type of *political system*; or
(3) the management or *control* of something.
Power...politics...control. None of those choices sound like
the kind of dynamic that ought to be operating in a vibrant
kingdom body of believers!

It would be much easier to simply not deal with church
government. In fact, as we've already discussed, a growing
number of believers are opting out of any organized church
experience. In doing so, they are answering the
governmental question. For them, there is none! But part of
the role of the church is to govern, and government is a gift to
the church.

"If a man's *gift* is...*leadership*, let him *govern* diligently."
--Rom. 12:6, 8

The Greek word here is 'proistemi', which means to stand before (in rank), to preside, maintain, be over, to rule. This implies significant authority. The word for diligently is 'with speed; eagerly; earnestly.' The role of governmental leadership according to the New Testament is not mere facilitation or just being one of the brothers. It involves focused, earnest, diligent leadership. Church government is given specific charges, such as directing the affairs of the church (1 Tim. 5:17). The spirit and manner in which this government is expressed is key. But in spite of potential misuse, godly government is God's gift to the church.

Having said that, let's continue to set delegated authority in its proper context by looking at the types of government that are very relevant to building kingdom churches.

God's Government

The yoke for the believer is easy, and his burden is light. Confusion comes most often in the area of government when we attempt to take on God's role. The privilege and responsibility of governing must always fall squarely on the shoulders of Jesus:

> "...the government will be on *his* shoulders." --Isa. 9:6

The eyes of the church in the West have been too low. We have been watching (and critiquing) how men administrate leadership in the church, but we have often failed to see "the God behind the man." God is in charge! He is ruling, and He may or may not choose to use human instrumentation in His own government. It is clear from the Scriptures that He uses people to govern. But all the while, He is the one governing us, and He wants us to "only have eyes for Him." Jesus promised to build *His* church (Mt. 16:18), and therefore we must look to Jesus and trust Him to complete what He has started (Heb. 12:2). He is our Source for everything! As much as we decry spiritual abuse and top-heavy church government, we as believers in the West have a tendency to want to follow in the footsteps of Israel in the days of Samuel by encouraging men to usurp the place only God is meant to fulfill:

> "All the elders of Israel gathered together and came to Samuel at Ramah. They said to him, 'You are old, and your sons do not walk in your ways; now *appoint a king to lead us*, such as all the other nations have.' But when they said, 'Give us a king to lead us,' *this displeased Samuel*; so he prayed to the LORD. And the LORD told him: 'Listen to all that the people are saying to you; it is not you they have rejected, but *they have rejected me as their king*.'"
>
> --1 Samuel 8:4-7

A core issue of repentance in the Western church is the fact that we have turned our eyes away from Jesus and have put them on human forms of church government too much, for too long. The answer is not to fall into typical all-or-nothing behavior and ditch all church government. God is building a people who, in the midst of proper human administration, keep their eyes fixed squarely on Jesus Christ. They know who their King is, and they are therefore able, *for the Lord's sake*, to submit themselves to every God-given form of government among men (1 Pet. 2:13). As we focus on the kingdom, we will see the church with peripheral vision, and as we focus on Jesus, we will see church leaders with peripheral vision as well. This is not disrespectful but appropriate and right.

Leaders, too, must strongly repent for not recognizing that it is really God's authority working *through* them and sometimes *in spite of* them. The plantation mentality operating in many churches in the West dictates that everything must pass beneath the head leader and/or board. Healthy people who do not have a need to control anyone make the best leaders. Their egos do not demand the church to focus on them. They continually point people to God and refuse to be a King in anyone else's life. Decision-making is done on their knees, in the fear of God.

In the book of Judges, Abimilech had a desire for leadership that was unhealthy, manipulative, and dangerous. He not only sought to be a kingly leader, but he also rose up against the established authority and killed 70 of his brothers. But there were 71 brothers, and the youngest brother, Jotham, hid from his older half-brother Abimelech to avoid being slaughtered. Later, Jotham stood before all the people and told a parable to the citizens of Shechem and Beth Millo to illustrate the difference between good leaders and ambitious ones. In Jotham's parable recorded in Judges 9, he likened people to trees and healthy leaders to olive trees, fig trees, and grapevines--all fruitful in their own right. But those leaders who are insecure, ambitious, controlling, and willing to have others bow before them are likened to a thornbush:

> "One day the trees went out to anoint a king for themselves. They said to the olive tree, 'Be our king.' But the olive tree answered, 'Should I give up my oil, by which both gods and men are honored, to hold sway over the trees?' Next, the trees said to the fig tree, 'Come and be our king.' But the fig tree replied, 'Should I give up my fruit, so good and sweet, to hold sway over the trees?' Then the trees said to the vine, 'Come and be our king.' But the vine answered, 'Should I give up my wine, which cheers both gods and men, to hold sway over the trees?' Finally all the trees said to the thornbush, 'Come and be our king.' The thornbush said to the trees, 'If you really want to anoint me king over you, come and take refuge in my shade; but if not, then let fire come out of the thornbush and consume the cedars of Lebanon!'"
>
> --Judges 9:8-15

Healthy leaders have no desire to "hold sway" over others, but ambitious leaders create dependency on themselves ("come take refuge in my shade"). In kingdom churches, God is truly in charge as the only King and Jesus really is the Head of the Church. Kingdom leaders are unwilling to become kings in anyone else's lives. Without a trace of false humility, they point people to Jesus.

God gives authority to people in the church to bring government and leadership, all the while expecting them to have the right heart posture of humility that would never usurp the place in people's lives reserved for God alone. This is a stewardship and an entrustment given to leaders to walk in the government of God without becoming a king over people. Jesus said that we should let people see our good works *in such a way* that they would glorify our Father in heaven. It's not that our good works are unseen. People will see leaders, but they will see Jesus beyond them. Leaders lead, but they lead veiled behind the government of God.

John the Baptist understood this dynamic when he called himself "a friend of the bridegroom." He wasn't personally married to the bride nor trying to get anything from her. He was an ally of the authentic Bridegroom and always acted in a manner that pointed people to Jesus. At one point, John even said, "He must become greater and greater, and I must become less and less" (John 3:30). This is the heart posture that allows God's government to flow in and through human vessels freely and without agenda or control.

Self Government

The first human realm of functional authority within God's government is self-government. Self-government means that every Christian is regulated by the Holy Spirit through the fruit of self-control (Gal. 5:23). The phrase "a kingdom of priests" speaks of people who have direct dealings with the God of heaven. Priests of the Lord hear from God and do what He tells them. They have an unmediated relationship that creates self-government. This is a restoration of the direct, unmediated relationship God enjoyed with Adam and Eve in the garden before the fall. It is available to God's sons and daughters who are indwelt by the Holy Spirit and who follow His inclinations.

David explained this principle of self-government in Psalm 32 when He spoke of God's intentions for His people:

> "I will instruct you and teach you in the way you should
> go; I will counsel you and watch over you. *Do not be like*
> the horse or the mule, which have *no understanding* but
> *must be controlled* by bit and bridle or they will not come
> to you." --Ps. 32:8-9

Clearly, a mediated relationship of control is not God's heart or first choice for His people. Only through a lack of understanding does the church chomp down on a bit and a bridle. We are designed for His gentle voice to lead us, not external controls. Circumstances, extra incentives of the Holy Spirit, and additional input from church leaders beyond what should normally be needed can all become God-allowed bits and bridles in our lives.

When Paul was concerned about whether or not he would be able to walk in integrity before God and man, he didn't first go to his pastor for counsel. Nor did he go to his small group and confess his sins, relying on his small group leader to tell him what to do. While both of these are fine to do at the right time, we are addressing the priority of self-government over other forms of human government in the church. Paul took personal responsibility to self-govern His life:

> "...I do not fight like a man beating the air. No, I beat my
> body and make it my slave so that after I have preached to
> others, I myself will not be disqualified for the prize."
> --1 Cor. 9:26-27

Through the decades of the 60s, 70s, and 80s, the culture of self was built in America like the tower of Babel, and the church has suffered greatly amidst self-centered attitudes. Much of the American church has created codependent ways of operating and relating to itself. Where there are codependent relationships, usually there is some form of benefit to the parties involved. The upside of codependent relationships is that there is plenty of room for blame and victimization. In a church culture of victimization, no believer really has to take any responsibility for themselves when they can blame the church. "If only the message was more anointed, if only someone had called me when I was hurting, if only they had better programs for my children"...on and on and on. While there are legitimate criticisms of most churches (Jesus corrected 5 of the 7 churches in Revelation 2 & 3), a lot of the problem has been a lack of self-government and an unconscious attempt to replace the authority and responsibility of every believer with a codependent relationship towards church leadership.

The Apostle Paul tapped into the internal power of God through the Holy Spirit and placed His flesh in subjection to the Holy Spirit inside of him. Because we live under the New Covenant and the Holy Spirit dwells within every believer, we have every resource in heaven we need to walk in self-government. It is not the church's job to govern individuals in these ways. This is the privilege and responsibility of each individual believer. We are called to become self-feeders in God's Word, to be individuals of prayer and the presence of God, and to initiate our fellowship and follow-up needs, and to minister with His authority. We have the power of God to govern and control ourselves in the Holy Spirit!

The Government Of Voluntary Mutual Submission

When I was being trained in church growth principles, the local church was essentially likened to a fish tank. Those leaders with large, beautiful 250 gallon fish tanks would gather a bunch of local pastors with 10- and 20-gallon fish tanks. There, we would learn how to break the 20-gallon "growth" barrier. We would find out that in order to break the 20-gallon growth barrier, we needed to have a better filtration system, more interesting rocks, some fish that would serve full-time to clean and care for the tank, and so on. Like thousands of other pastors in North America, I was under the assumption that my goal was to get a bigger and bigger fish tank. What I didn't realize is that whether the fish tank was 20 gallons or 250 gallons, it was still just a fish tank, with glass walls and a glass ceiling. We've heard of the glass ceiling in business. Most churches are not aware of the glass ceiling (and glass walls) that exist in their thinking, structure, attitudes, and views towards the members of the church. Members of churches can never experience the freedom of the kingdom when they're in a fish tank.

Then I came to realize that the context of the church was never meant to be in a fish tank at all. It was meant to be in an ocean! In the ocean, there are endless possibilities and many significant dangers. But there are no walls and no glass ceilings. There is freedom to swim and play and explore! Discovery is returned to the fish, and the joy of "fish without walls" is experienced!

How you handle yourself isn't quite so important when you're in the fish tank. Everything is governed for you. You can be rebellious and swim over in the corner if you want, but ultimately, the fish tank manager will make sure you get your food and the tank is cleaned. But how different it is in the ocean! There, choosing to be independent could cost you your life! Survival and well-being are often found in schools. Fish voluntarily swim together out of instinct because they know it is the best way for them to survive and to thrive. (And it's more fun!) Together, dolphins can take on a shark, but alone, they are vulnerable.

This is why voluntary mutual submission is a superior form of government to top-down forms of control. The wineskin of the past provided safety and predictability, but with limited experience, surprise, and discovery. Kingdom churches are full of endless possibilities because the people are in the ocean, not a tank. They understand and gladly yield to mutual submission and relational accountability. It is vital for the health of the church, and it originates from the place of love, respect, and care for one another. Church government has often been about submission to a leader, a board, and/or a staff who were responsible *for* you. In kingdom churches, we submit to one another out of reverence for Christ. Leaders in kingdom churches are approachable and correctable along with everyone else. While we give honor to whom honor is due, and we lavish love on one another because of Christ, we don't treat anyone like a king...except Jesus.

> "They are defying all of Caesar's decrees, saying that there is another king, *one* called Jesus." --Acts 17:7

Church Government

When God's government is truly recognized and Jesus is the only King in the church, when each believer is empowered with the understanding of self-government, and when mutual submission permeates the atmosphere, we can then (and only then) turn our attention to the subject of human leadership in the church.

For many people, church has meant hoops to jump through and men to cower before. There has been an ungodly emphasis on structure, authority, submission, and titles which lends itself toward the fear of man, a man-pleasing spirit, and favoritism.

While structure, authority, submission, and offices are all taught in scripture, church leaders throughout history have all too often embraced a wrong, fleshly understanding of these things that, left unchecked, gravitates towards inappropriate control. Even two of Jesus' own disciples, James and John, seemed to have regular difficulty with the use and expression of the Lord's authority through them. At one point, they asked Jesus if they could occupy places of ultimate authority and power by sitting on either side of him in heaven! A bold request to be sure. On another occasion, when some people didn't submit to their leadership and provide a proper welcome for Jesus, they asked Jesus if they could call down fire from heaven to destroy them! In both instances, Jesus expressed disappointment in their attitudes and corrected them.

Correcting our understanding will involve more than just learning how to smile or be nicer when we exert control. It will mean more than *trying* to value people that don't directly contribute to building our church's vision. This is a major paradigm shift that calls for and embraces mutual submission, equality in the body, and the priesthood of all believers--wherever we find them--as practical realities, not simply theoretical ones.

When will we know that we have made this shift? When we see people in the light of love, we will find our hearts honoring every other believer regardless of how they benefit us. Our mind won't be going a thousand miles a minute trying to figure out how we can fit them into our plans. We will enjoy them and silently ask God how we can be a blessing to them. We will experience in our hearts a genuine sense of honor for others, and we will no longer see one another in relationship to how they fit in the church's pecking order. Their value and our investment in them will have more to do with the leadership of the Holy Spirit than our hasty and often shallow conclusions based on hierarchy.

SPHERES OF AUTHORITY

Having set a proper perspective for types of authority and government, we can now look at the human reality of spheres of authority as it relates to building kingdom churches. Spheres of authority have to do with who has what authority when and where and for what purpose. It is the practical outworking of authority in the church.

Paul refers to these *spheres* (also called *fields* in the NIV) when he addresses the Corinthians:

> "We, however, will not boast beyond our proper limits, but will confine our boasting to *the field* God has assigned to us, *a field that reaches even to you*." --2 Cor. 10:13

In this passage of Scripture, Paul discusses assignments from heaven for those with God-given authority. Paul lays out three key principles in verse 13. First, it is about a field that has limits and definition. Second, our ministry sphere is assigned by God. And third, it is about people. In verse 15, Paul calls it his "area of activity" and in verse 16, he refers to it as a person's "territory." Of course, he is not simply referring to "turf" or physical geography, but rather he is discussing God's call on his life to specific people, cities, and nations. Peter clarifies the reality of this "sphere" in 1 Peter 5:2-3 when he addresses the job of church elders:

> "Tend--nurture, guard, guide and fold--the flock of God that is [*your responsibility*]...those *in your charge...*" [AMP]

The NASB tells leaders to "exercise oversight...over *those allotted* to your charge", and the NIV says to "be shepherds of God's flock that is *under your care*...those *entrusted to you*." This is key. God has made certain leaders stewards with authority who have a specific group of people entrusted to them. These people make up their sphere. Of course, that sphere can grow or be redefined by God over time. The point is that it is a defined group of people in God's heart that is entrusted to those with authority.

This has implications for those who have been entrusted with authority, and it has implications for those who are meant to be within the sphere of someone else.

Mission And Ministry

Jesus had both a *ministry* and a *mission*. In Luke 4:18-19, Jesus boldly and clearly declares his ministry manifesto:

> "The Spirit of the Lord is on me, because he has anointed me to *preach good news to the poor*. He has sent me to *proclaim freedom for the prisoners* and *recovery of sight for the blind*, to *release the oppressed*, to *proclaim the year of the Lord's favor*."

Jesus announces the activity of the kingdom that will occur through His life. He will go here and there, bringing God's kingdom and ministering in the love and power of God. People will receive good news, there will be healings, miracles, and salvations. People will rejoice. In Acts 10:38, we see a summary description of the result of this kind of kingdom ministry:

"...God anointed Jesus of Nazareth with the Holy Spirit and power, and how he *went around doing good* and healing all who were under the power of the devil, because God was with him."

Jesus went around doing good. This is a *ministry*. It is not necessarily tied to a specific, local group of people. It is not a relational sphere but a geographic one. It is a ministry based on anointing, gifting, and calling and can happen anywhere within God's designated geography for a person. It is well-suited to travel. Jesus ministered as He went.

His *mission* was actually quite different. He was totally committed to reproducing his life in the ones given to Him by the Father. He called these ones his disciples, and then later, his apostles. In His High Priestly prayer to the Father, Jesus refers to these twelve men as a specific *entrustment* to Him from the Father (17:6, 9, 12). In that regard, in John 17 Jesus didn't intercede for just anyone but specifically for those men. He reported back to the Father how He had watched over them, protected them, taught them, and loved them. Before He left the earth, He spent time in prayer asking the Father to protect those specific men.

This was His mission, and He completed it. Jesus passed on his spiritual DNA to some specific men. He made disciples, especially with twelve, and then also with seventy. He then gave this same commission to them and to us in Matthew 28:18-20, popularly known as the Great Commission (or Co- Mission)--to invest in the specific people that God gives us. This same principle is found in 2 Timothy 2:2.

Every believer has been given both the *ministry* of Jesus (to bring the kingdom of God everywhere they go and especially in their designated geographic sphere) and the *mission* of Jesus (to make disciples in their specific relational sphere and to watch over them with love and care). Because this is the mission of every believer, it should not surprise us that God has designated specific people in the church to have God-given delegated authority for the mission of caring for and watching over churches. This is a *good* thing!

Outside The Camp?

Many believers today are confused by this issue of sphere. They don't want to "come under" another person's "covering," so they avoid Biblical spheres altogether--to their own detriment. This is often especially true of those who are seeking to establish ministries "outside the camp" of the local church. This phrase, "outside the camp", has grown in popularity as a way to communicate one's disdain for and avoidance of interaction with anything that looks like the "organized" church. But the New Testament reference to "outside the camp" in Hebrews 13:11-13 has to do with God's people going outside the camp of the pagan culture in which we live to bear the reproach of being Christians. It has nothing to do with Christians going "outside the camp" of the rest of the church as a self-appointed group of elite believers or as an anointed lone ranger. This is not God's heart. Spheres are Biblical.

Often because of pain and misunderstanding, sincere, anointed believers will start ministries that embody part of Jesus' purpose on the earth while avoiding any relationships that involve submission to authority. They go around doing good. They are bringing God's kingdom, traveling, speaking, ministering. They may start itinerant ministries or open ministry centers. If they are prophetic, then they may prophesy and teach on prophecy. If they move in deliverance, they may speak on deliverance, hold weekends devoted to deliverance, and do prophetic counseling. But they have difficulty coming into someone else's sphere, often because they have failed to recognize, honor, and submit to the reality of these relational spheres.

Governing And Equipping

There are two basic spheres of authority given in the New Testament: governing and equipping. The governing sphere of authority has to do with caring for people and having responsibility (and authority) to watch over them. This sphere is referenced in Hebrews 13:17:

> "Obey your leaders, and submit to their authority. They keep watch over you as men who must give an account."

The equipping sphere of authority has to do with the God-given roles listed in Ephesians 4:11 to strengthen and equip the church so it can come into a place of maturity. Governing and equipping spheres combine in kingdom churches to release kingdom authority. While the purpose of this book is not to provide lengthy definitions of these roles, we will look briefly at each type of sphere.

Governing Spheres. The New Testament identifies three governmental roles in the church: *apostles*, *elders*, and *leaders*. A survey of the New Testament will bear out the fact that all reference to church rule and the submission of God's people have to do with these three roles. *Apostles* are those sent by God who have unique authority to establish churches, to set in place the foundational elements of a given church, to appoint elders, to exercise discipline, to impart gifts, and, depending on the arrangement of the local church, to exercise apostolic oversight over a church or group of churches in a geography or network. Usually for at least part of their ministry, apostles establish churches and then move on, but it is also Biblical and appropriate as the Lord directs for apostles to remain as primary leaders in a local or city church, such as James in the Jerusalem church. *Elders* have authority to watch over and shepherd the flock, to teach, to model the Christian life, and to exercise rule in the form of counsel, correction, and even direction of the overall body. Elders always function in a plurality and are the primary governing body in a local church. *Leaders* is a general term to describe those who exercise oversight of and provide direction for ministry arenas and tasks. Apostles and elders are also leaders, but not all leaders are apostles and elders, as there are other kinds of leaders. Contrary to popular teaching today that everyone can be a leader, the Bible says that leadership is a specific gift from God that not everyone has (Rom. 12:8). Leaders are to govern diligently in their spheres.

Equipping Spheres. Ephesians 4:11 identifies five equipping roles in the church: *apostles, prophets, evangelists, pastors,* and *teachers.* While there are many gifts listed in 1 Corinthians 12, Romans 12, 1 Peter 4 and so on, the gifts listed in Ephesians 4 describe five functional roles for equippers in the body of Christ. These five kinds of gifts have authority to equip and build up the church and are to be recognized and honored as having such authority. This set of ministry functions, often referred to as the "five-fold", comprise a specific equipping arena both in local churches and also in the larger body of Christ.

Gift Mix. While these distinctions of governing and equipping are important for developing a Biblical paradigm for kingdom authority, the reality is that most of God's people have been given more than one gift or talent. Therefore, someone who is a prophet may or may not also have been given the gift of leadership. In Acts 15, Judas and Silas were referenced first as leaders (15:22) and then later as prophets (15:32). Here we see the reality of gift mixes, where people operate in multiple roles based on their God-given gifts.

The Local Church

I believe that a basic Scriptural principle is that every believer is meant to be part of the sphere of a local church. Psalm 68:6 says that God sets the lonely in families. Every believer is meant to be part of a local church family. The goal of Biblical spheres of authority should not be to rule or lord it over anybody but to serve the church and to equip the saints. Likewise, the goal of each believer should not be to act independently but to walk in mutual submission and to minister interdependently in concert and partnership with others.

In the next chapter, we'll continue this subject by taking a fresh look at how kingdom authority functions in and through the leadership of kingdom churches.

Chapter Six
Kingdom LEADERSHIP

"Also a dispute arose among them as to which of them was considered to be greatest. Jesus said to them, 'The kings of the Gentiles lord it over them; and those who exercise authority over them call themselves Benefactors. But you are not to be like that. Instead, *the greatest among you should be like the youngest, and the one who rules like the one who serves.* For who is greater, the one who is at the table or the one who serves? Is it not the one who is at the table? But I am among you as one who serves.'"

--Luke 22:24-27

Kingdom leadership is unique among the various leadership styles on the earth and in many respects is the exact opposite to its worldly counterpart. It is the highest and best style of leadership. In fact, more than a style of leadership, what Jesus is talking about is a type of person to whom God entrusts servant leadership among His people. The eyes of the Lord search throughout the whole earth in order to strongly support a person whose heart is completely His (2 Chron. 16:9). In the days when King Saul disqualified himself from his position of leadership, God describes his own leadership search to His prophet Samuel when he says, "I have found...a man after my own heart..." (Acts 13:22). Leaders in kingdom churches reflect the heart of God and walk in a way that looks like Jesus. In this hour when the church is radically changing, God is looking for kingdom leaders after his own heart.

CHARACTER AND SKILL

One of my favorite verses about kingdom leadership is found in Psalm 78:72, where King David's leadership in Israel is described:

"And David shepherded them with integrity of heart; with skillful hands he led them."

This combination of heart and hands, of integrity and skill, is key for kingdom leaders. King David, perhaps the greatest political leader, military commander, and spiritual songwriter in the history of the nation of Israel, was described by Asaph in this Psalm as having these two balancing aspects of character and skill.

Here we see a Biblical glimpse into David's greatness, as well as a pattern for all Christian leaders who are called to lead and care for people. This verse, like many in the Psalms, is a Hebrew parallelism, in which the author describes the same or similar activity with overlapping word choices to provide a more beautiful, poetic, and accurate way of expressing a multi-faceted truth. In this case, the truth is leadership, and the Psalmist Asaph gives us two overlapping concepts about leadership: shepherding with integrity of heart, and leading with skillful hands.

The reality is, we don't simply lead with great training. We lead with our hearts, hearts of integrity. Put more directly, integrity leads people. And then, so do skillful hands.

Shepherding With Integrity Of Heart

Shepherding in Hebrew is "ra`ah" and refers to "tending a flock, pasturing it to graze, to associate with as a friend, to keep company with." It is the *relational* aspect of leadership. The word rendered here as "integrity" comes from the root word "tom" and means "completeness, innocence, perfection, simplicity, uprightness, cleanness, being completely spent on behalf of another." Heart ("lebab" in Hebrew) really is simply the "most interior organ" and can also mean our courage, our understanding, the place where passion resides.

Leading With Skillful Hands

Leading means "to guide, to bring, to govern, to lead and put forth, to transport somewhere." "Skillful" in this passage is the Hebrew word "tabuwn" and refers to our intelligence, discretion, reason, understanding, cunning, discernment, instructiveness, knowledge, perceptions. Hands is the word "kaph" and simply means the literal hollow part of the hand or palm. God gives His leaders skill to govern and lead.

Some Christian leaders gravitate toward either heart or head, toward either fruit or gifts, toward either *leaderless care* or *careless leadership*. But there's no need to have to choose! This verse, along with the understanding behind these important words, demonstrate a model of leadership that involves both heart and hands, fruitfulness and giftedness, character and skill, servanthood and leadership. It is this balanced model of leadership that we are pursuing in kingdom churches.

A Fluid Model

Kingdom leadership has more curves than square edges. It has more overlap, more shared leadership, and is derived from a more fluid rather than static model. It is depicted best not by a pyramid, where top-down authority works best, but by a flock of birds, where leadership changes hands based on the objective, or by a network, and where true partnership occurs. It's about team and mutual submission versus command and control, and yet leaders do, in fact, guide and govern. It's about servanthood in the context of partnership and mutual honor. Kingdom leadership always empowers rather than disables the unmediated priesthood of all believers. Any leadership model we embrace must accomplish this.

APOSTOLIC LEADERSHIP

At various times in church history, God has breathed on truths in the Scriptures in a pronounced way. His ability to highlight what has always been there causes us to rediscover important revelation that we had previously not understood properly. Jesus came to earth in what Paul terms "the fullness of time" (Gal. 4:4). In similar fashion, God is releasing in the Western church a fresh revelation of New Testament roles during this time before the return of Christ. In particular, there is at this time in history increased revelation and understanding on the subject of apostolic leadership. In the past, we have looked through various lenses for our understanding of Biblical leadership principles. In this season I believe it is essential that we understand and embrace an apostolic ethos and an apostolic leadership model in kingdom churches.

Currently, there is more and more being revealed and written about apostolic leadership, because God is allowing us to understand all leadership through apostolic lenses. For numerous reasons, I believe it is essential that we come into a place of real understanding about what it means to be apostolic and how this matters in the churches that we build. To that end, I want to bring some definition to what I believe are the three most important aspects of apostolic leadership: (1) the *evidence* of apostolic ministry; (2) the *activity* of apostolic ministry; and (3) the *heart* of apostolic ministry.

Keep in mind that as we discuss apostolic leadership, we are looking for the Biblical truths that are applicable today and not solely reserved for the Lamb's twelve (Rev. 21:14). These select men had unique authority and a special call that cannot be duplicated. However, there are apostles today with a small "a", and God is desiring to release encouragement to His entire church to become apostolic in its nature and expression. The word itself, "apostle," simply means sent one. God desires all believers to be apostolic or missional in our orientation, because according to Matthew 28:18-20, we have all been sent! Because apostolic leadership is essential to build kingdom churches, it is very helpful to understand and embrace the role of apostles today and the nature of apostolic ministry.

The Evidence Of Apostolic Ministry

When we're wondering what is truly apostolic and what is simply a word on a business card, we must see clear evidence or proofs of apostolic ministry. The activity and heart of apostolic ministry, which we will look at in a moment, are also evidences in a broad sense. But there ought to be three particular evidences accompanying ministry today that is apostolic or claims to be. Jesus commends those who understand His requirements for apostleship and then judge accurately by those standards (Rev. 2:2). Some teach that there are dozens of different kinds of apostles and prophets. This teaching has a tendency to greatly broaden and unnecessarily complicate the terms and their definitions. I don't know if the Scriptures support these complex definitions or not. Personally, I believe God defines His terms in simple, clear, and understandable ways. When it comes to the evidence of apostolic ministry, I believe all three of the following evidences must be present in order for us to be accurate when we call someone an apostle.

New Believers. Paul wrote to the church in Rome that he was given grace to be an apostle "to call people from among all the Gentiles to the obedience that comes from faith" (Rom. 1:5). In 1 Corinthians 9:2, Paul reinforces this evidence when he says, "Even though I may not be an apostle to others, surely I am to you! For you are the seal (i.e., stamp of authenticity) of my apostleship in the Lord."

Again, Paul told the Thessalonian believers that they were his "joy" and his "crown." The evidence, joy, and reward of apostolic ministry is changed lives and, in particular, new believers brought into the kingdom of God. Anyone who is truly apostolic will have changed lives in his or her wake, including new believers.

New Churches. Apostles lay foundations and set things in order. They are not fond of building on another man's foundation but are wired to start things--in particular, churches--by bringing the gospel to new areas (Rom. 15:20). Apostles aren't building just any ministry. They are planting and building *churches* (1 Cor. 3:8-11). After laying apostolic foundations, they insure elders are appointed and that churches are properly cared for (Titus 1:5).

Signs & Wonders. Again, Paul is very plain about a third evidence of apostleship in 2 Corinthians 12:12-- "The things that mark an apostle--signs, wonders, and miracles--were done among you with great perseverance." These are evidenced in Paul's ministry as he brought the gospel (Rom. 15:19). Modern-day apostles regularly move in the supernatural as an evidential sign of their God-given apostolic ministry and authority from God.

A person can plant and pastor a church without being an apostle. People can win others to Christ and they are not necessarily apostolic. And a gift of healing or miracles does not make someone an apostle. But where the combination of these three evidences exist, the likelihood of apostleship increases. In addition to these three evidences, apostles engage in key activities as well.

125

The Activity Of Apostolic Ministry

Acts 6:1-7 is a very instructive passage for understanding what the activity of apostolic ministry is about. In the midst of a church management crisis, it becomes clear that a team is needed to oversee the food ministry. Without any misgivings or false guilt, the apostles do not come under the pressure to provide pastoral care or administration. Instead, they articulate the job description as they passed on this responsibility to another group of servant-leaders while they remained true to their primary activities:

> "It would not be right for us to neglect the ministry of the word of God in order to wait tables. Brothers, choose seven men from among you who are known to be full of the Spirit and wisdom. We will turn this responsibility over to them and will *give our attention to prayer and the ministry of the Word*" (Acts 6:2-4).

Apostolic activity centers around two primary activities: (1) being with God in private and public prayer and intercession, and (2) the ministry of preaching and teaching God's Word both for the purpose of evangelizing the lost and for equipping the saints. Apostolic leaders are drawn to the realm of prayer and the ministry of God's Word, whether in small or large settings, one-on-one and in crowds, among the lost and among the church.

The evidences and activities of apostolic ministry must be in place for someone to be an apostle, but at the core of what I want to talk about is the apostolic heart. This is really the part that is most transferable in our understanding of kingdom leadership.

The Heart Of Apostolic Ministry

My favorite description of apostolic leadership is found in 1 Corinthians 4. This chapter, written by the apostle Paul, describes the nature, character, and heart of true apostolic ministry. Paul articulates *four vital aspects* of the heart of apostolic ministry that characterized his own life and ministry and that I believe are meant to characterize all apostolic ministry and really every kingdom church today.

Servants of Christ (4:1). The heart of apostolic ministry is servanthood. Apostles are not trying to take over--although others might perceive them that way! They realize they have been given great authority from God, but they are constantly using that authority to build people up and to make others great (2 Cor. 13:10). Paul vigorously defended his "right" to be an apostle so that others might receive his ministry to their own benefit. He fought hard with churches to "prove" his authority, all so he could turn around and lay down his life on their behalf.

As a young believer I was excited to learn that God had placed a large call on my life and significant authority in my hands. Then I read Jesus' words in Luke 22:24-27 about how the greatest must become a servant. With fresh resolve, I figured that I would pay the price and go through a season where I really learned how to serve. This would then release me and qualify me to come into my true calling as a leader with great authority. So I worked as an usher, sweeping floors and setting up chairs. I worked in other varied ministry positions, mostly in a "servant" versus leadership capacity. Over time, I began to move into positions of authority and leadership, until finally I was released and commissioned to become a senior pastor at my very own church! I was so excited. At the beginning of this time, as I entered into "full-time" paid ministry, a very reliable prophet spoke to my wife and I, explaining that God wanted to take us from where we were to a place where we became servants of all. He essentially prophesied the Luke 22 passage over my life. With even more resolve, I figured God wanted to take me through another phase where I learned about servanthood even more. Greatness and destiny would soon follow.

I don't remember when exactly it occurred, but not too long after becoming a recognized leader I had an epiphany. Suddenly, I realized that servanthood wasn't a phase that we pass through to get where we're going. It is the destination. God wants to help all of us become "great!" In order to do that and to reach our full potential of ministry, we must become servants, not as a phase we go through, but as a permanent place of residence! Servanthood isn't a means to greatness. Servanthood is greatness. This is meant to be true for all believers. And certainly, servanthood is at the heart of all true apostolic ministry.

Stewards of a mystery (4:1-8). Paul's entire orientation was that God had given him the greatest treasure, the Person of Christ, who dwelt in the earthen jar of his body. This mystery of Christ in us as our entire hope of glory was something that Paul was thrilled to release to others. He saw himself as a steward, someone who had been entrusted with truth and reality of incredible value that he was glad to give away to the people in his God-given sphere.

When apostles come to others, they do not come to take. They come to give. They know that they are full of a mystery, and as good stewards, it is their responsibility before God to give this mystery of Christ away. As carriers of God's glory and as servants, they are constantly trying to help others come into their destiny. They see themselves not as anointed masters but as childlike messengers, bringing fresh bread from heaven and dispensing it among the people. Apostles are those who have been entrusted by God to unfold the mystery of Christ to the people in their spheres. It is required of a steward that he be found faithful, and apostles are faithful to "preach Christ crucified" (1 Cor. 1:23). In order to keep their message pure, apostles keep the focus on the Person of Jesus. Again, Paul said, "For I resolved to know nothing while I was with you except Jesus Christ and him crucified" (1 Cor. 2:2).

Spectacles of men (4:9-13). Apostolic ministry has a stigma of misunderstanding attached to it. People whom Paul loved and laid his life down for were constantly misunderstanding Paul's motives and devaluing his authority. For example, Paul spent significant time in the books of 1 and 2 Corinthians trying to lovingly convince the Corinthians that he was the real deal and that they needed to listen to him! He summarizes this dilemma in 1 Cor. 4:10 when he says:

> "We are fools for Christ, but you are so wise in Christ! We are weak, but you are strong! You are honored, we are dishonored!"

Having worked in the building industry, and in particular in foundations and framing, I know personally that foundation work is not glamorous. It is dirty, hard work that doesn't draw the wows of people like, say, the work of the interior decorator does. Apostolic ministry is about making sure foundations are right and things are set in order. It is, in many ways, the "grunt work" of the building process! But it is also extremely important. God is raising up apostolic leaders who are secure enough to be hidden, who are rooted in the love of God so much that they are OK with the fact that many don't understand or recognize the place they occupy in the Spirit or the price they pay by standing in the gap for others.

Because God has given apostles great authority, he requires a very high degree of death. Every believer is called to lay down his life and follow Christ, but where there is great authority, there is great responsibility. Paul told the church of his close association with death when he said this:

> "I die every day--I mean that, brothers--just as surely as I glory over you in Christ Jesus our Lord." --1 Cor. 15:31

John Wimber used to say, "Never trust a leader without a limp." This was a reference to Jacob, who wrestled with the angel and found his hip put out of socket for the rest of his life. It also refers to the need to qualify leaders based on their brokenness before God and their humility before men. It is impossible to truly be "apostolic" without truly being dead! God entrusts great authority to dead people--those who have died to their own aspirations and have become voluntary bond slaves dedicated to building the kingdom of God and not their own ministry. Others may have anointing that makes them look apostolic, but death to self is a major requirement for and mark of true apostolic ministry.

Spiritual fathers (4:14-21). We live in a "fatherless", latchkey generation, and the concept of someone acting as a spiritual mentor to us, or of us acting in that role with others, is hard to grasp for many. Most of the protestant church has steered clear of the concept of spiritual fathers and mothers. The abuses that came out of the "shepherding movement" have caused the church to overreact and avoid the issue of healthy mentoring in the church altogether. Even our own trust issues come up when we think of trusting a spiritual father, or much less of asking someone to trust us to help them in their lives. We have much to overcome!

In his book, <u>The Father Heart Of God</u>, Floyd McClung agrees:

> "So many people are orphaned, not just from their physical parents, but from any kind of healthy spiritual or emotional heritage. The church is filled with spiritual orphans. Either...they have not been nurtured in their faith, or...they have not become a part of a spiritual family...They need a spiritual father or mother who can help them grow in the Lord. Others need to be 'reparented'...if proper parenting was missing during a person's developmental years...he or she needs someone to provide an example.
>
> Being a father or mother in the Lord is not limited to those who are pastors or spiritual leaders. There is also a very crucial need for other spiritually mature, caring people to act as 'fathers' and 'mothers' to other believers. By their very presence, they minister to those around them because of their maturity and depth in God. We need to turn loose these 'moms and dads' in the church to be who they are."

Paul boldly declared himself to be a spiritual father both to individuals, as in the case of Timothy and Titus, and also to entire churches, such as the churches in Corinth and in Thessalonica (1 Tim. 1:2; Titus 1:4; 1 Cor. 4:17; 1 Th. 2:11).

This apostolic mandate of spiritual fathering and mothering is an essential part of kingdom leadership and a defining characteristic of the apostolic heart. Again, there are many who display powerful anointing and do great ministry. But until we are willing to lay down our lives and invest in other people, rolling up our sleeves and being vulnerable emotionally to the point where people can trust us as spiritual parents, we will never move from anointed to apostolic. The ministry of apostle is about investment in people--not from a distance, but with those we relate to personally.

APOSTOLIC COMMUNITIES

God is raising up apostolic communities, which we are calling "kingdom churches." These kingdom churches operate under an apostolic ethos. They are led by apostolic leaders or at least have the regular influence of apostolic ministry in their midst. The *culture* of these churches is apostolic. They are characterized by the nine primary traits of an apostle. Of course, God isn't just wanting to release apostles. He wants the entire church to be apostolic, communities that are missional in their orientation. Here is a summary list of what we've just looked at:

1) transformed lives and people coming to Christ
2) planting new churches as expert builders
3) supernatural power in signs, wonders, and miracles
4) significant time in prayer in private and in public
5) preaching and teaching to the lost and to the saved
6) servants who focus on ministering to and blessing others
7) stewards who give away & unfold the mystery of Christ
8) spectacles who bear the stigma of misunderstanding
9) spiritual parents who father children and churches

If every member of every church laid down every title and position they had and focused solely on becoming a living demonstration of these nine apostolic traits, we would be on our way to revolution! In America, we are continually seeking new ways to *organize our way into revolution*. But it's about becoming, about embodying the realities of the kingdom. These traits are the heart and essence not only of all kingdom leadership but of all kingdom people!

Strong Leader, Strong Team

Some years ago I was in a meeting where Jim Goll introduced the term "apostolic team ministry" (ATM for short). Although I never heard Jim teach on this subject beyond the introductory comments in that meeting, I always sensed in my heart that he had captured in a phrase something very significant for our understanding in the years to come.

Someone has said, "You cannot strengthen the weak by weakening the strong." As the church is experiencing a radical shift in many of its paradigms, there is often an unconscious "dumbing down" of leadership and strongly gifted people. Because we desire the priesthood of every believer so strongly, we must be especially cautious of devaluing strong, healthy leadership. If you have a strong leader and a weak team, you have the same old pattern of overly controlling leadership that dominates. Equally true is the fact that if you have a strong team but a weak leader, you have a committee! (And they certainly don't exist in the Scriptures.) I believe there is coming a healthier model of strong leader and strong team, where everyone on the team is honored and valued, no one feels intimidated, and leadership is present but it functions in life-giving ways so everyone stands shoulder to shoulder and advances together in strength.

More Authority, Less Control

Kingdom churches experience *more authority* but *less control* through their leaders. As the Lord continues to restore apostolic authority to the church, we may begin to hear news of modern-day Ananias and Sapphira moments! When Peter spoke to this couple in Acts 5 about their deceit, he was operating in spiritual authority from heaven. It wasn't about church or structure or politics or control. It was about the kingdom authority Peter carried in the Spirit to discern what was needed for the moment and to pronounce God's temporal, corrective judgments within the church. Think about that. Peter spoke, and people died! But the result of Peter's use of authority was not others bowing down before him. Instead, more than ever, believers fixed their eyes on God as "great fear seized the whole church" (v. 11). In fact, even unbelievers and God-seekers were affected with a holy reverence for God and His people (v. 13). The final result of seeing kingdom authority expressed through the church was that more and more people believed in the Lord, and the company of believers grew (v. 14).

When kingdom authority functions in the church, the result is reverence, respect, and repentance. Control is not needed in such an environment. Everyone's eyes are on Jesus, the atmosphere is filled with holiness and the fear of the Lord, and humble submission and godly honor are the only logical heart postures of everyone in the church. There are no superstars in kingdom churches. Instead, there are like-minded people who have entered into covenant relationship and who have chosen to walk together in love. Leaders are those who simply occupy a role and fulfill a ministry that is no less than or greater than anyone else's. There is so much mutual honor and heart-felt appreciation for one another that the fear of control dissipates. Perfect love casts out fear! When there is tension over leadership, I am learning to call out to God for more love! I believe we need greater love to walk in greater authority and more Biblical realms of leadership.

The Role Of Kingdom Leadership

As kingdom churches emerge with a strong emphasis on the priesthood of every believer, mutual submission, self-government, and so on, the nature and role of leadership must change to fit this new wineskin. This change will be especially tough for pastors who do not have apostolic gifting. Pastors of existing institutionally-oriented churches are already beginning to feel the tension of a paradigm shift (and the accompanying loss of power). In the past, there were always those to blame for this tension--the rebellious crowd that is always bucking authority. But now, the massive shift that is occurring is so widespread, it is so pervasive, that it cannot be dismissed with such shallow analysis.

An entire generation of new leadership is taking shape! Those who have been leading under an older, modernistic framework will soon have a very important decision to make: (1) Will I hold my ground, remain unwilling to change, and vilify those who are calling for change? (and eventually leaving 'my' church); (2) Will I see my role as pastoral while also recognizing the need for apostolic leadership on our church, and make needed changes? or (3) Will I allow God to transform me into a new kind of apostolic leader--even though I don't quite know what that will look like?

All of this begs the question: What is the role or job description of a kingdom leader, and how is that different from what most church leaders are currently doing?

What Kingdom Leaders Aren't

There has been plenty of deconstructionism over the last decade, so I don't want to spend a lot of time on this, but let's look for a moment at what kingdom leaders aren't. When we describe these characteristics, we are not saying that some of these roles aren't appropriate. A large church may need on its staff some of these roles! However, the leadership of kingdom churches, and in particular a point person, is *not* described by the following:

Managers. It is not the primary job of kingdom leaders to manage but to lead. Management (i.e., stewardship) does need to take place and is a valuable role, but it is done by others who have a gift to manage.

Controllers. It is not the job of kingdom leaders, nor has it ever been, to control anyone. Leaders lead, and people follow. Leaders empower, and people are free to run!

Pulpiteers. Preaching and needed, especially when it is anointed and in the streets! But professional pulpiteers who find identity and spend all their time attached to a pulpit (or preparing to be attached to it) have difficulty leading kingdom churches.

Priests. The priesthood of every believer cannot flourish if there is a dominant priest to whom everyone else looks. We are all priests with unmediated relationships. The role of caretaker belongs in the homes of the wealthy, not in the church! Nor should leaders be dumping grounds for others.

Encyclopedias. We have paid experts to research and spew out answers to our questions, to our own detriment. I deeply appreciate well-learned teachers of God's Word, but kingdom leaders are not given by God to be expert answer men.

Who Kingdom Leaders Are

This is by no means exhaustive, but here are a few key roles of kingdom leaders that matter and must be valued:

Pray-ers. Kingdom leaders are focused on the simplicity and purity of devotion to Christ. They have more faith in God's ability than their own. They go to their knees before they do their jobs, because going to their knees is their job. They bathe everything in prayer continually (Phil. 4:6; 1 Th 5:17).

Imparters. Kingdom leaders live out of the overflow. They have a vital connection with God that results in a "splash" on everyone else. They are eager to give away what God has given them. They love to leave kingdom imprints everywhere! They love to give fresh, hot bread and empower others to reach their destiny in Christ (Rom. 1:11).

Models. It's not OK to just be a pointer: "There is the way." Jesus said, "I am the Way." Paul said, "Imitate me." We are called to be models (2 Thess. 3:9). We must be and do what we want to see. The messenger is the message. We embody the message. We are living epistles--our lives preach.

Catalysts. Kingdom leaders are firestarters, forerunners, and catalytic people who influence others by their internal fire. They are change agents without a whole slew of methodology. Instead, they rely on the Spirit's presence and power. Like John the Baptist, they are burning lights (Jn. 5:35).

Voices. Kingdom leaders create culture and shape paradigms. They help people to see and celebrate the kingdom and find Jesus. They are cheerleaders for kingdom success. They give voice to the things on God's heart. God-ordained kingdom leaders are not leaders because they have a voice, but rather they are a voice because of who they are and what they see (Isa. 40:3).

LEADERSHIP SCENARIOS

I believe the primary issue we face today in transitioning into apostolic leadership is that most of our churches are led by individual pastors without the plurality of elders or the influence of apostolic teams. Biblically, pastors have an equipping role in the body of Christ and have been gifted by God to train the saints in the ministry functions of listening, counseling, prayer, inner healing, deliverance, relationship, shepherding, and care. While these functions are extremely important, they are not the best gift mix to lead a community of faith significantly larger than a home fellowship (unless the person has a strong leadership gift as well). The crisis of pastors leaving the ministry is a testimony to this fact. They are not built for the job they are being required to do.

Every kingdom church needs apostolic DNA in its leadership. How this occurs is secondary. Sometimes, an apostle leads the church. In other cases, an apostle or apostolic team plants the church, turns it over to elders, and then visits periodically. Sometimes, there is an apostolic network of churches where each church is led by a spiritual father & mother (elder couple) and the apostolic team cares for these leaders and churches.

On a practical level, a good understanding of apostolic leadership provides a backdrop to discern healthy church scenarios for a given people at a given time. Because leadership is a fluid model and is based on objective rather than position, there are actually a variety of ways to structure kingdom churches. Factors include the size of the church, the age of the church, who is willing and available to lead, and the sovereign call of God on the church itself.

Kingdom Leadership In A Brand New Church

God must be the one who starts churches, not man. If people collectively decide to start a church on their own, without the heavenly mandate, I believe the church itself is out of order. Will God use it? Yes. Will God bless it? If the gospel is being preached, yes, He will bless it. But, as with everything else in the Christian life, the good is the enemy of the best. In this free-wheeling era of spiritual entrepreneurship (and I am hugely in favor of spiritual entrepreneurship!), it is important for us to know that we were "sent" versus we "went!" Sending is modeled continually in the book of Acts, a loose handbook for church planting. Of course, we are first sent by God, but even Barnabas and Saul, whom the Holy Spirit clearly sent, were commissioned by the other leaders at Antioch. When they had preached the gospel and planted the church, they reported back to the leadership there in Antioch.

I believe apostolic ministry should be involved in the birthing process of every local church. Apostles started churches in the New Testament, and apostles released other ministry roles, such as elders. In places where churches are rapidly reproducing, apostolic ministry can partner with the local 'pastor', elder or team to birth the church and turn it over right away to local, indigenous leadership.

Kingdom Leadership In A House Church

Clearly, house churches are growing in popularity in the West, as they should. House churches are thoroughly Biblical and are a refreshing alternative to many larger traditional churches which have become institutional in their orientation. I believe house churches work best when they are led by an elder couple like Priscilla and Aquila (1 Cor. 16:19) who serve as spiritual father and mother to their flock. This is eldership in action, defined by function rather than as a position on a board.

Because house churches are relatively small and are usually focused on shared leadership, any of the five equipping roles (apostle, prophet, evangelist, pastor, teacher) could also lead/facilitate a house church. As long as there is reasonable care and 'one another' ministry, the type of gifted person leading the house church is not as mission critical. The important thing is that the flock is cared for while remaining connected to something bigger than itself so that apostolic influence is constantly injected in the DNA. *House church networks* are emerging as a viable model of church life. These networks provide the best of all worlds in that, the leadership of the church is eldership, but the network has apostolic influence. I believe God is breathing on this model of church life at this time.

Kingdom Leadership In A Community Church

The average and most common church size in America is somewhere around 70 people. Why is this so? I believe a primary reason is because for centuries, we have built churches around the pastoral gift almost exclusively. Good pastors (with lots of energy) have an ability to effectively care for around 70 people. If the church gets larger than that, people begin to lose touch with the pastor. And when they no longer feel connected to the pastor, often they leave to find something that better meets their needs.

Community churches that range in size from about 35 to 200 people and that remain centered around a solo pastoral couple are not wrong or bad as some are saying today. We must simply recognize them for what they are. They are essentially home churches that meet in a building and sit in rows rather than a circle. If the style of leadership involving a primary pastoral couple is working for the people, then I say, more power to them! Personally it is not my favorite kind of church, but that's OK, because God likes all the people involved, and He will bless them!

Over the coming years, I believe many community churches will change the way they operate. As more and more senior pastors of community churches are quitting the ministry due to unfulfilled expectations and burnout, I believe many community churches will either (1) change from pastoral to apostolic leadership and grow; (2) join forces with another church; or (3) disband. Many leaders who were originally created to be apostolic and who have settled for pastoral roles are currently being called by God to make a *leadershift* from pastoral to apostolic. This move of God will revitalize the community church scene, and we will see fresh releases of apostolic authority coming on seemingly stalled community churches. God will redeem everything for His glory!

Kingdom Leadership In MegaChurches

In my opinion, almost every growing megachurch is led by either a highly gifted evangelist, an excellent teacher, or more often an anointed apostle. It would indeed be rare for a true prophet (and I love prophets!) to be a megachurch point person because they're usually too vertical (and combative!), and true pastors (and I love pastors!) usually don't lead megachurches because they're not wired for the pressures of hundreds or thousands pulling on them.

Nearly every healthy, growing megachurch has multiple layers of leadership that involve all or nearly all of the New Testament leadership gifts. Whatever gift the senior leader has, usually he has surrounded himself with complimentary gifts on his staff. There are also usually designated elders and small group leaders, so the church is flowing in most of the essential gifts in the New Testament. A great megachurch is incredibly valuable.

Kingdom Leadership In Cities And Regions

When you combine these various kinds of churches in cities and regions, you get a more complete picture of kingdom leadership. Citywide and regional eldership begins to emerge. These are the pastors of house churches and community churches. An apostolic council can emerge, made up of those apostles of megachurches, along with apostolic church planters and others who have apostolic authority in a region. The equipping ministries of Ephesians 4:11 become translocal consultant gifts and servants to the churches in the region as they exercise their function and equip the saints for the work of ministry, sometimes through city or regional ministries, such as houses of prayer, training schools, healing rooms, prophetic companies, and so on. As walls between local churches continue to fall, we will see new city and regional networks emerge.

LEADERSHIP STRATEGY

As we bring this chapter on kingdom leadership to a close, I want to offer a few thoughts about our strategy that may be of some help to those who are either desiring to build a kingdom church or who are desiring to refine their current leadership paradigm.

Governing And Equipping

We introduced the concepts of governing and equipping in the previous chapter. As I look at the New Testament, I see the governing roles of apostles, elders, and leaders, and I see the equipping roles mentioned in Ephesians 4:11 of prophet, teacher, pastor, evangelist, and apostle. I believe both governing and equipping roles are vital for building kingdom churches. If the church is large enough, all these roles can exist in the church. If it is a smaller church or a house church, all these roles can exist in the apostolic network of churches within the city or region. The point is that the cross-pollinization of governing and equipping roles is very powerful in unleashing healthy, balanced kingdom life.

Governing roles are leadership by *context*. This means that the sphere of ministry has to do with people and the various contexts in which they gather. Equipping roles are about leadership by *objective*. The objective is to minister to people and to equip the saints for the work of ministry.

Governing roles may be expressed, for example, as leaders of cell groups or house churches, with department leaders overseeing various aspects of larger celebrations. These are all contexts for ministry. Equipping roles are less recognized in traditional churches but vital for their well-being. Equipping roles express themselves by the objective at hand. A prophet wants to prophesy to the people for their benefit, and he also wants to equip others to prophesy.

These are two very important objectives. They are not based in a particular context but fueled by Biblical direction.

In many churches, there is difficulty trying to understand how these different kinds of roles express themselves. For example, in a board-run church that only recognizes the authority positions of small group leaders and department heads over contexts (like the director of children's ministry), a gifted prophet will have difficulty finding expression and will probably have to lead a small group in order to find ministry expression and role validation. However, in a kingdom church, both governing gifts and equipping gifts are honored. This means that the church is not dominated by administratively gifted people, but instead there is a healthy balance of gift and ministry expression.

When you embrace both governing and equipping, there is great grace and multiplication.

To provide a visual picture, we map out our leadership structure in a matrix-style chart. The boxes across the top represent generalists who govern and ministries that represent

JESUS! oversight	Kingdom COMMUNITIES	Kingdom CELEBRATIONS	Kingdom DISCIPLESHIP	Kingdom RESOURCE
PROPHETIC Team				
TEACHING Team				
PASTORAL Team				
EVANGELISM Team				
APOSTOLIC Team				

what others may call "programs", but what I call *ministry by context*. The boxes down the left side represent specialists who equip. These are what I call *ministry by objective*. My desire is to help provide a leadership strategy for these diverse calls to intersect so we experience fullness in our local church.

In our local community called Everyday Church, we are developing a leadership team that includes what is commonly referred to as the "five-fold" alongside of overseers of major ministry areas. This combination of governing and equipping is powerful.

The blank boxes in this matrix-style chart represent the places of dynamic kingdom intersection. For example, our prophetic team has the objective to release prophetic ministry while also equipping people to prophesy in each of the four contexts listed at the top of our chart. We work together as a team to discern Holy Spirit goals, and then we move towards those. At this time, our prophetic team is working within our kingdom celebrations to provide a prophetic presbytery at our weekend gathering. Once this is functioning, we will seek God for our next objective.

This combination of strong leader / strong team releases unlimited potential. We communicate to the people who make up our church, "The church changed the moment you showed up." In other words, because we are interdependent, our ministry depends on who God brings us. Therefore, our objectives are determined by the Holy Spirit and confirmed by the people He brings. This is truly team versus program. And it's working.

Jesus is over everything! Human oversight is represented in the box under Jesus provided for the sake of unity. Our government is made up of three teams: the leadership team, which is all the leaders in the boxes I already mentioned (and includes elders); the financial team, who steward resources; and the oversight team, who provide external apostolic input and protection.

What about the "senior pastor"? The term "senior pastor" is not bad or wrong as many are concluding today, but it can be confusing and is probably not always helpful. When it describes the point person among a plurality of elders who shepherd God's flock, then I believe it is accurate. When it is used to describe one who leads a team of pastoral equippers a la Ephesians 4:11, we are also using the term correctly. Ephesians 4:11 is the only place in the instructional epistles where the word "pastor" (gr. *poimen*) is actually used of people besides the Lord Jesus. Those we commonly refer to as "pastor" or "senior pastor" may really be people who have the dual role of *governing* as a lead elder and of *equipping* the saints as an Ephesians 4:11 pastor. For these reasons, we prefer other terms. If the point person leading a church is apostolic, it might be more appropriate to call him a "senior leader", a "lead strategist", or something like that. The primary point is that we want to build a DNA of team into our churches that includes both governing and equipping. We want to use terms that don't overshadow or inhibit the proper use of the diverse governing and equipping roles but instead release them.

Our leadership strategy is unique, in that it is based on the call of God on our local church. I do believe, however, that the principle of cross-pollinating governing and equipping can be translated into any context so that they become useful to every kind of kingdom church, from house churches to community churches to megachurches.

As we describe a paradigm for church planting and building here in the West, we must always be aware that such paradigms are only "scaffolding." Someone once said, "when revival hits, all bets are off!" We hold our strategies with a loose grip, holding tightly to Jesus instead. We invest in people rather than programs. Our strategy gives us a "track to run on", and we also feel great liberty to divert from the track at any given time. It is wonderful dynamic that we are exploring together.

In the next chapter we're going to take a look at gathering contexts for ministry and how they can flourish in kingdom churches.

Chapter Seven
Kingdom GATHERINGS

"Therefore go and make disciples of all nations, baptizing them in the name of the Father and of the Son and of the Holy Spirit..." --Mt. 28:19

It is very exciting that the Church in the West is finally hearing the call of Jesus to "go." The church huddled is turning into the church mobilized. God's people are growing restless with platform-driven Christianity, mostly confined and mostly defined by the default setting of meetings. We are bored with meeting after meeting, where much is talked about but little is actually done. As one song goes, "You're not some dead god who lives in a building..." Christianity was actually never meant to be an indoor sport! Finally the world and the church are bored with the same thing! Good riddance to the days of the immobilized church focused on itself through repeating services.

The holy discontent that has been brewing for some time is beginning to produce churches without walls. Kingdom churches are made up of missional people who are not meeting-centered. These fiery missionaries are keenly aware they are on a holy assignment from God to infiltrate society with the gospel of the kingdom. Their Biblical center is not platform ministry but everyday Christianity lived out in our homes, among our neighbors, at work, school, and in the marketplace. Jesus modeled a life on the streets and out among the people. His ministry was effective and a model for all who live under the New Covenant.

As this holy emphasis on organic Christianity continues to build into a tidal wave of nameless, faceless believers bringing the gospel of the kingdom to every facet of society, we will find ourselves rejoicing more in the church "scattered" than in the church "gathered." This voluntary and purposeful scattering will enable more people to hear the gospel and meet the King than if we had stayed together and simply enjoyed our meetings.

Don't get me wrong. The early church had lots of gatherings. In fact, the early church in Jerusalem collectively met together every single day, both in smaller contexts (houses) and in larger venues (the temple courts)--cf. Acts 2:46 and Acts 5:42. This wasn't just a unique phenomenon limited to the church in Jerusalem. Paul recounted a similar gathering dynamic in Ephesus, where the assembled church gathered in houses to facilitate smaller groups, and outdoors, evidently where larger groups of Christians and unbelievers could gather (Pauls calls this "publicly" in Acts 20:20). The early church clearly gathered often, though gathering didn't define them.

Gatherings are not the problem, per se. In fact, gatherings are Biblical when in their proper proportion. While the "go ye" command is primary in kingdom churches, there is a secondary call to gather together as the people of God for encouragement:

> "Let us not give up meeting together, as some are in the habit of doing, but let us encourage one another--and all the more as you see the Day approaching." --Heb. 10:25

Kingdom churches are dynamically fluid. They enjoy a wonderful balance of coming and going, of gathering and scattering. Creating this dynamic is the assignment given to kingdom servants:

> "Then the master told his servant, 'Go out to the roads and country lanes and make them come in, so that my house will be full." --Luke 14:23

This verse captures the dual "go ye, come ye" mandate given to the church. The church mobilized is the army, seeking and saving the lost, one person at a time. Those individuals are then brought into something--the house of God. While this "house" in Luke 14:23 is spiritual and doesn't in any way imply a building, the term "house" does speak of a large community of people ("that my house may be *full*"). Psalm 68:6 declares that "God sets the solitary in families." The church gathered in community simply represents the family, into which God brings the solitary.

The Church Is A Group Of People

While most believers understand that the Church universal includes all who trust in the Lord Jesus Christ alone for salvation, many Christians today are starting to agree again with the New Testament that a viable expression of church happens whenever believers come together. In fact, that number can be quite small, "where two or three come together" in the name of Jesus (Mt. 18:20). But that same passage of Scripture in Matthew 18, which earlier deals with correction, tells us that there are certain matters that are to be told to the church (Mt. 18:17). This text implies that there was a recognized and defined group of people to whom these matters could be told. A similar dynamic is described in Acts 14, when Paul and Barnabas returned to Antioch from their missionary journey and wanted to give a testimony to their sending body:

> "On arriving there, *they gathered the church together* and reported all that God had done through them and how he had opened the door of faith to the Gentiles."
> --Acts 14:27

Whether large or small, what is commonly called the local church is, in fact, a defined group of people that make up a subset of the larger body of Christ called the universal

Church. Although it may be limited in cases of extreme persecution, part of what it means to be the church is to gather. And, since this is true, the subject of gatherings has great significance for those attempting to build kingdom churches with excellence. What are we to think of gatherings? How often should we gather, and for what purposes? How do we meet as local expressions of the church in small and larger contexts? What about the church in the city, or the church in a region? And what "family" lines should and shouldn't be drawn at this time in order to build with a new set of kingdom eyes? These are the kinds of important questions that are worth reconsidering as we build kingdom churches.

GATHERING CONTEXTS

The subject of Christians gathering together is becoming a "hot potato" in the church. For as long as I can remember, a primary litmus test for being a committed Christian has been faithful attendance at a Sunday morning church service (or whenever the church has its main service/services). Nevertheless, there is an increasing boredom and restlessness in the hearts of many of God's people with these services, well-intentioned though they are. While pastors are exerting effort to encourage people to "show up" at these services, more and more Christian people are growing disinterested in and even ambivalent towards attending Christian gatherings-- and especially the Sunday service. To be sure, some of these restless ones struggle with structure in general and have problems with commitment and authority. Yet there are others--sincere, godly, submitted, committed believers--who feel that something is missing, though they might have trouble articulating what that is. Confusion comes because they know there are good things happening in these services, and they feel guilty for not being more excited about what they are experiencing.

There are a few key complaints that are repeatedly leveled at the main service/services, which we are calling "the Sunday morning service." Here are five primary complaints:

The church is IMPERSONAL. As a service grows and becomes larger than a hundred or so, this complaint is increasingly heard. People come and attend an event, but inside they are hungry for relationship. Therefore, the longer they sit and listen, filing in and out of a building each week, the longer they start to feel disconnected, especially as the church grows.

The church is a 'ONE MAN SHOW.' Many Christians understand that God has given them spiritual gifts. They know there has to be more than one person in such a large crowd that has something to say, and yet we only get to hear from the same one person over and over. The church is longing for the body to be the body, where we get to see many gifts in operation and many people making contributions. Sitting in a pew on Sundays seems to perpetuate consumer, spectator Christianity, and many Christians are finding themselves less willing to perpetuate this.

The church is BORING. Because we design services to contain certain elements, they quickly become predictable. This tends to breed boredom and frustration as people pretty much know what is going to happen. The surprise is long gone, and so is expectancy. Once a person has been a believer for several years, this boredom increases, because they have now heard hundreds of sermons often on the same topics or scripture texts, sung the same songs hundreds of times, and greeted thousands of people over the years. The sheer repetition alone can cause boredom, and coupled with the predictability, boredom is pervasive. People sometimes come to church services more out of duty than delight, and many can't wait until it's over.

The church lacks POWER. As more and more of the church is getting in touch with God's presence & power on a personal level, they expect to see and feel the same in gatherings. Many believers are having experiences with God, and when they come to 'church', they expect to have continued experiences with God. For a variety of reasons, many services tend to lack power and experience. People don't encounter God in services the way they want to.

The church is too INWARD. Once a church reaches a comfortable level, either in size or in vibe, and the founding or majority members are satisfied, there tends to be a lack of desire or effort to reach out to new and lost people. The sad result is that over time the church doesn't seem to care as much if anyone new shows up. For many visitors, going to a new church is like breaking into a high school clique, and fewer believers are willing to do that in church.

For these and other reasons, the Sunday morning church service (or its equivalent) has become a dividing line for a growing segment of Christians in North America. People are no longer willing to simply show up, be quiet and behave. This quiet revolt speaks of the need to take another look at gatherings from a kingdom perspective.

Having said that, it must also be stated that Sunday morning church services have become the perfect scapegoat for all that is wrong with the church in North America and the West! In any organization, often the most visible elements become universally responsible for the problems of the whole, because they are easiest to see and point the finger at. While God is revolutionizing many aspects of His church, not all of what He is doing is aimed at the Sunday services. Often, what's wrong in the Sunday service is simply a symptom of what needs to change in the overall vision and expression of the local church. The issues at stake are larger and deeper than simply reformatting church services to be more interesting, inclusive, or culturally relevant.

God's people gathering together is a Biblical practice, modeled and encouraged as part of both the Old and New Covenants. But that is not the end of the story. Assumptions about gatherings have been passed on from generation to generation of church goers, resulting in mind-numbing repetitiveness and, at times, a cool detachment from the vibrancy of New Testament Christianity. The paradigms and practices we have built our churches around are currently subject to adjustments by the Holy Spirit. As my friend Gary Goodell says so eloquently, "Permission has been granted to do church differently in the third millennium."

Changing The Center

Sunday morning services in particular have become an *idol* in our church expression in the West. I am not advocating the removal of all Sunday services. Rather, I am definitely advocating the removal of their centrality in our thinking and practice. While weekly Sunday services can be convenient to have because of the cultural expectations in the West, we don't actually need these services to accomplish our mission of bringing the gospel of the kingdom to humanity. Nor do we need them to accomplish our mission of changed lives. Even though Sunday services are culturally convenient, they are also incredibly labor-intensive, and the effort put into many Sunday services across America is not always worth the results. Sometimes our Sunday services are underwhelming. Can you imagine a highly impacting, growing church in North America without a Sunday service (or its equivalent)? I can, because they are emerging in many places. Furthermore, Sunday mornings are becoming a great time to either gather as house churches or, better yet, for believers to spend time with unbelieving neighbors and friends for the sake of evangelism!

A growing number of God's people are beginning to embrace *the value of the church scattered over the church gathered.* For those of us who are used to thinking of and defining the church in terms of its gatherings, this shift, while easy to talk about, is much more difficult to embrace and to put into practice--especially for church leaders.

Let's face it. Regardless of rhetoric to the contrary, the center of most churches in the West is the platform that is used at our main service/services, whether that is Sundays, Saturday nights, or Tuesday nights. For centuries, we have been developing platform-centered church life. Because we have been putting so much emphasis on the Sunday service and other gatherings, we have developed a built-in consumer mentality that is now coming back to bite us. The value shift from the church gathered to the church scattered is a difficult one for paid professionals to make. We have made a large part of the job of the senior pastor (and the staff) to provide a fantastic service for the people, filled with great worship and dynamic preaching containing amazing alliterations and excellent exegesis. And once pastors do that, plus some counseling and some leadership development, what else is there time for?

At some point, the platform is no longer adequate to be the center of organic church life, and a values shift must take place that redefines how we view and practice gatherings. The focus and attention of the church is moving from 'come ye' to 'go ye', and our identity is shifting from the church 'gathered' in meetings one or two days a week to the church 'scattered' in the marketplace, living courageously for Christ everyday and viewing the mobilized church scattered throughout the community as our most consistently valid expression of Christianity, far more important than church services.

Beginning in Acts 8:1, with the onset of the persecution of the church, we get a Biblical glimpse into the value of the church scattered: "On that day a great persecution broke out against the church at Jerusalem, and all except the apostles were *scattered* throughout Judea and Samaria." But because the early church in Jerusalem kept the focus of the church outward and missional, when the involuntary scattering occurred in Acts 8, they didn't miss a beat.

"Those who had been scattered preached the word wherever they went." --Acts 8:4

The very next story in the narrative describes Philip being led by the Spirit into the streets to preach the gospel. Later in the story, he speaks with the Ethiopian eunuch. Philip leads him to the Lord, baptizes him, and then Philip gets transported to another town where he preaches some more, all the while rejoicing! This is not the behavior of a man concerned with when he was going to go to his next church service! This is a kingdom man who lived among an outward, missional people.

The effectiveness of the gospel multiplied exponentially when the church was scattered. The gospel went from a single city (Jerusalem), to places such as Phoenicia, Cyprus, Antioch, Pontus, Galatia, Cappadocia, Asia, and Bithynia (Acts 11:19; 1 Pet. 1:1). Modern-day examples, such as the house church movement in China, provide ample evidence that the church scattered, without the benefit of a platform-driven model of church life, flourishes.

Kingdom churches embrace each individual as a priest of the Lord. Therefore, there is great confidence in the church scattered. Kingdom churches value the church scattered over the church gathered, because it is as the church is scattered that we can model Jesus and impact society. The church gathered, when considered central to the definition of the church, becomes a holy huddle, irrelevant to the society around us and inward in our orientation. When the gathered church is considered central, our money and efforts reflect this thinking, and we are then forced to pursue larger buildings and staffing to accommodate the larger gathered crowd. The work required to pull off our gatherings can tax God's people to the point where our services are getting in the way of the church scattered. It's not about a particular size church but rather a focus on Sunday services or other large gatherings that becomes the sum total of the church's experience and effectiveness for most people in the church.

By contrast, when this value of the church scattered is central, with a focus on the kingdom of priests, all church gatherings take a step down in importance. We can only reasonably consider how to come together when the backdrop of the church scattered is in place and visible in the discussion.

It is evident in both Old and New Testament times as well as through early church history that God's people gathered in a variety of settings, depending largely on the level of persecution: indoors and outdoors; in living rooms, synagogues, temple courts; on mountains, in caves, in valleys; in prayer meetings and preaching services; with and without food present; in upper rooms and catacombs; and so on. With the exception of a few prescriptive passages, such as 1 Corinthians 11-14, the New Testament essentially contains descriptive rather than prescriptive language about gathering contexts. Therefore, there is a lot of liberty for kingdom churches to meet wherever and whenever! Other factors come into play that call for wisdom, discernment, and Holy Spirit 'intuition' (skills also required for good fishing!), such as what works best culturally and geographically.

Two Primary Biblical Contexts

The church has gathered in the two primary New Testament contexts of smaller groups and larger assemblies at various times throughout history. For example, before 1960, small groups were not very popular in the U.S., but since the charismatic renewal began in the early sixties, small home meetings have been springing up for about 40 years now and have become a standard context for many churches in the West. Whether you call them small groups, cell groups, G12s, house churches, or some other name, collectively they represent one primary Biblical context. I like the term "Kingdom Communities" because it describes the essence of these gatherings without prescribing a certain format. At our church, we have developed a hybrid model of smaller meetings that we describe like this:

> "Kingdom communities are people in relationship who are pursuing God's presence and advancing God's purposes together in the spirit of friendship. They vary in size (3-30), age (youth, adult, mixed), gender (men's, women's, mixed), duration (ongoing or for a period of time), type (house churches, groups, teams, clubs, etc.), and emphasis. Join one (or several)!"

Of course, in addition to these smaller settings, the church gathers in larger contexts. In the early part of the book of Acts, this gathering place was either at the Temple or outdoors in crowds. Today, these gatherings are often called "Sunday services" or "celebrations." The early church clearly gathered in both of these primary contexts:

> "Every day they continued to *meet together* in the *temple courts*. They broke bread *in their homes* and ate together with glad and sincere hearts" --Acts 2:46

> "...all the believers used to *meet together in Solomon's Colonnade.*" --Acts 5:12

> "Day after day, *in the temple courts* and from *house to house*, they never stopped teaching and proclaiming the good news that Jesus is the Christ." --Acts 5:42

> "You know that I have not hesitated to preach anything that would be helpful to you but have taught you *publicly* and from *house to house.*" --Acts 20:20

The New Testament record indicates that preaching, praying, and participatory edification were happening in both smaller and larger contexts.

We all know that the church doesn't consist of a worship service one day a week, but of a people who walk with God in the midst of their ordinary, everyday lives. We are the church! And we are learning to "be" the church, carrying God's presence and power wherever we go and whatever we find ourselves doing. Then, when we gather at various times during the week, there is great joy in His presence as we enjoy each other and share together in a way that edifies & equips one another.

So why do we go to church services, anyway? Even though we are focused on *being* the church rather than *doing* church, there is still great value in being together in larger corporate settings. Here are four reasons why being together makes sense, both Biblically, historically, and practically:

1. To *worship* God in the company of the saints.

In Psalm 35:18 David declared, "I will give you thanks in the great assembly; among the throngs of people I will praise you." While it is true that we can worship God wherever we are, there is a spiritual dynamic released when God's people assemble and release extravagant devotion to Him. It is good and right to bring our offering before the Lord in His assembled "house." This offering is more than finances. It is our heart, our gifts, and our prayers. It is the heritage of God's children to bring their personal offering to God into the company of other believers.

2. To *encounter* God in the company of the saints.

We call our services "Encounter God Celebrations." This is because people regularly encounter God! Again, we can encounter God privately, but because of the unusual manifest presence of God available to us when we gather (Matt. 18:20), personal encounter with the beautiful God is a reason to gather, both for saints and for lost people. Encountering God provides the bridge between the saved and the lost and settles the seeker question. Everyone needs to encounter God. Church isn't an event. It is a Person. We want *everyone* to encounter Jesus.

3. To be strengthened in Christ.

When the body comes together, we experience the fullness of gifts in operation, which releases fullness of strength. 1 Cor. 12 speaks of the vital necessity for all of the gifts in operation when we come together. In particular, the five equipping gifts of Ephesians 4:11, released in the assembly, edify the church and equip the saints for the work of ministry. The preaching of God's Word is a powerful, God-given tool to strengthen the church. So is mutual ministry according to our gifts.

4. To help others come to know Jesus.

When the early church gathered, the result was that people invariably became Christians! As the church experienced God's power, the lost were attracted and saved, from Pentecost in Acts 2 onward. Paul instructed the charismatic Corinthian church to gather in a way that helped the unsaved come to know Jesus Christ (1 Cor. 14:24-25). This is still a worthwhile reason to gather.

Of course, the core issue of our gatherings must be about the *dynamics* that happen when we gather rather than the particulars of the gathering itself. And the Scriptures do have something to say about gathering dynamics!

GATHERING DYNAMICS

There are some key Biblical principles that will help us define the purpose of our meetings with much more clarity and help us discern what is meant to occur in gatherings of kingdom churches. Let's look at four principles that are essential to consider when preparing for and building great kingdom gatherings: (1) Biblical Participation; (2) The Role Of Preaching; (3) Planned Spontaneity; and (4) The Dwelling Place Of God.

Biblical Participation

There is a strong Biblical basis for more participatory gatherings than we have grown accustomed to. These practical guidelines are given to us in 1 Corinthians 14. The context of Paul's discourse to the church in 1 Corinthians 11-14 is captured in the phrase "when you come together", which is referenced 4 different times (11:18, 20, 33; 14:26). This is a passage of Scripture that is definitely instructive on gatherings, with much to say about participation. Let's take a fresh look at Paul's insights regarding Biblical participation in kingdom gatherings.

Our Basis. The basis for more participatory gatherings is woven throughout 1 Corinthians 14. Paul is indicating the involvement in the gathering of more than the worship leader, the announcement person, and the speaker. He not only says 'everyone' but then mentions various contributions. Paul repeatedly emphasizes multiple contributions during gatherings:

> "I would like *every one of you* to speak in tongues, but I would rather have you prophesy." (v. 5)
> "If an unbeliever or someone who does not understand comes in while *everybody* is prophesying, he will be convinced by all that he is a sinner and will be judged by all, and the secrets of his heart will be laid bare. So he will fall down and worship God, exclaiming, 'God is really here among you!'" (v. 24-25)

"When you come together, *everyone* has a hymn, or a word of instruction, a revelation, a tongue or an interpretation." (v. 26)

"Two or three prophets should speak, and the others should weigh carefully what is said. And if a revelation comes to someone who is sitting down, the first speaker should stop. For you can *all prophesy in turn* so that everyone may be instructed and encouraged." (v. 29-30)

Our Purpose. The purpose for participatory gatherings is two-fold: edification and evangelism. Our first reason for mutual contribution is for the benefit or edification of the whole church. Our goal is not simply self-expression [which is childish thinking, v. 20]. Paul always subjugates self-expression to the test of mutual benefit. In other words, it is not enough to have people contribute in a church gathering simply because they want to, or because they feel stifled. The goal and purpose is always for the greater good of the church. These contributions are for the benefit of others.

"For anyone who speaks in a tongue does not speak to men...but everyone who prophesies speaks to men *for their strengthening, encouragement and comfort*." (v. 2-3)

"He who speaks in a tongue edifies himself, but he who prophesies *edifies the church*...he who prophesies is greater than he who speaks in tongues, unless he interprets, *so that the church may be edified*." (v. 4-5)

"Now, brothers, if I come to you and speak in tongues, *what good will I be to you, unless* I bring some revelation or knowledge or prophecy or word of instruction?" (v. 6)

"Since you are eager to have spiritual gifts, try to *excel in gifts that build up the church*." (v. 12)

"You may be giving thanks well enough, but *the other man is not edified*." (v. 17)

"For you can all prophesy in turn *so that everyone may be instructed and encouraged*." (v. 31)

Our other reason for mutual contribution is for the salvation of lost people. Paul also puts evangelism above self-expression when he says in vv. 24-25:

"So if the whole church comes together and everyone speaks in tongues [which is generally for self-edification, v. 4], and some who do not understand or *some unbelievers come in*, will they not say that you are out of your mind? But if *an unbeliever* or someone who does not understand comes in while everybody is prophesying, he will be convinced by all that he is a sinner and will be judged by all, and the secrets of his heart will be laid bare. *So he will fall down and worship God*, exclaiming, 'God is really here among you!'"

Read in context, Paul is clearly saying that our purpose for the priesthood of all believers practiced in gatherings must include our desire for lost people to come to Christ. Our expression of gifts must be mindful of those with us who don't know the Lord. This principle would apply to any size meeting.

An exciting truth in this verse is that the multitude of gifts flowing in a church gathering is used by God to bring salvation to lost people! Perhaps our evangelistic efforts have been hindered because we've required one person (the pastor) to use all the gifts to help people get saved. Praise God for the day when we see unbelievers coming to our gatherings and finding Jesus because He is so clearly seen and heard through the prophetic contributions of so many of His people!

Our Guidelines. Guidelines speak of both what we release and how we evaluate what we've released in gatherings. We then use these Biblical guidelines to determine how to administrate participatory activity in our gatherings. We want to release all Biblical gifts of the Spirit, in their proper context, given through godly people filled with the Holy Spirit and in relationship, within the Biblical guidelines He has given us in His Word. There are specific gifts listed in 1 Corinthians 14:26 as appropriate for participation:

> *Singing:* A song offered to the Lord that builds up those who hear it. I would include dance & the arts here. This song could be planned (with music, on stage) or spontaneous.

> *A word of instruction:* This is not a full teaching, but a word. It is like a prophecy but from the Scriptures to instruct and encourage all who hear it.

> *A revelation:* This could be a word of knowledge, word of wisdom, dream, vision, picture, or impression. Given clearly and appropriately, this can be powerful.

> *Tongues with interpretation:* Tongues is worship in another language from man to God. It is not prophecy, but a word of praise to God. In the church, it must be accompanied by interpretation. [This does not prevent individuals from singing or praying in tongues softly within a church gathering. The guidelines apply to when the attention is purposefully on one person who is 'giving' a tongue for all.]

Especially prophecy (v. 1, 3, 24-25): Of the gifts listed, Paul singles out prophecy (speaking to others on God's behalf) as the most important and useful gift in church gatherings. He encourages us to eagerly desire to prophesy (v. 1). This would include general prophecy (v. 3), which involves speaking God's heart and mind (i.e., His present Word) for individuals and/or for the group gathered so that people are strengthened, encouraged, and comforted. This builds up the church! It would also include specific prophecy (v. 24-25), which involves speaking from God to another the 'secrets' of a person's heart (who may not know the Lord) so they can either come to Christ or be convinced of God's wonderful presence among us. It includes words of knowledge (i.e., 'secrets' revealed). This builds up the individual and in some cases causes the preChristian to repent and be saved!

Our Evaluation. And then there is evaluation. Once we understand the potential for powerful good that a release of God's Spirit in a gathering can be, we must also see the unfortunate potential for damage. Like a powerful river, there needs to be banks to steer or direct the 'flow' so that the power is used for God's purposes and not to distract or even damage the body in any way.

Few people feel safe when there are no guidelines and no facilitating leadership, especially when it comes to 'open' sharing that has a spontaneous element in larger gatherings. Thus, evaluating such activity is vital, since we are aiming for quality (i.e., beauty & excellence in worshiping Jesus Christ) as well as quantity (i.e., many people making contributions). In fact, we are commanded by God to 'judge' the contributions of others (1 Cor. 14:29). To judge here, or 'weighing carefully' (NIV) means 'to separate thoroughly, to discriminate, to call in question; to discern, to think, and to conclude.' The idea here is not to be judgmental, but to use discernment as you listen to others speak. As thinking, feeling people trying to learn how to release multiple contributions in a gathering, we want to help gently guard the quality of those contributions by using Biblical measurements to evaluate and give feedback. Here are the kinds of questions we use to evaluate:

> *Did it strengthen?* "All of these must be done for the strengthening of the church." (v. 26) Our standard for evaluation is whether or not the church is being strengthened. If it was revelation, was it accurate and fitting? If it was song or dance, did it draw attention to Jesus? If it was a word of instruction, did it help the majority of people in the room?

> *Was it for the whole church?* "...so that everyone may be instructed and encouraged." (v. 31) Some things are meant to be shared with a close friend. Some things are meant to be shared in a home and/or a small group setting. And some things are meant to be kept to oneself. We want to have things shared in their context that are meant for the whole church that is then gathered. This could include a prophetic word for an individual that blesses the entire church upon hearing it, or someone might have a word of knowledge that leads us to pray for a group of people within the church. As long as the whole church that is gathered is built up, it is appropriate.

> *Was it decently and in order?* "Everything should be done in a fitting and orderly way."

(v. 40) Biblically and practically, it means following the rules and rhythm of the gathering. If there is an atmosphere of joy and celebration, a rebuking word about repentance probably wouldn't be in order. Following the theme that seems to be established by the Spirit is important here and requires sensitivity. If there have already been a few prophetic words and the facilitator is closing that time, another prophetic word might not be in order.   Further, it helps to ask, is the contribution fitting with the philosophy, heart, and people of the church? Common sense, courtesy, and consideration work well here to help us find balance in these things, as well as making sure we are in relationship with each other.

Was it done in love? "Eagerly desire the greater gifts. And now I will show you the most excellent way." (12:31) Sandwiched between 1 Corinthians 12 and 14, the two greatest chapters on spiritual gifts in meetings, is 1 Corinthians 13, the greatest chapter on love. To exercise spiritual gifts in love means that our motive is truly to bless others rather than draw attention to ourselves.   It also means that we are not easily offended if others do not receive or appreciate our gifts or if we need gentle correction about the use of our gifts.

The opposite of loving contributions are those done out of "envy and selfish ambition" (James 3:14-16). These contributions create confusion and potentially invite trouble from the enemy! (cf. James 3:16) It is important that our contributions are from a heart of love than from a lesser motive.

Now, before we immediately qualify this message of participation as only applicable to small groups and home meetings, we'll want to notice that no such qualifications are given in the text. It is likely that the church in Corinth was a house church, where the complete household included anywhere from 20-50 people. However, the size of the church in Corinth is not clear. Some Bible teachers believe, based on circumstantial evidence, that the Corinthian church could have been several hundred or even several thousand people. What is clear is that large gatherings can (and should) include at least some expression of Biblical participation as outlined in 1 Corinthians 11-14.

The Role Of Preaching

On the other side of the coin, and equally evident in the Scriptural model and mandate of kingdom expression, is the place of one person preaching the Word of God to a group or crowd of people. Some who advocate egalitarian participation as the only legitimate activity in gatherings seem to have forgotten or ignored the many Biblical examples and exhortations towards Biblical preaching. They see preaching as some sort of "old wineskin." In light of the thousands of sermons many of us have heard, we might find ourselves agreeing with those Gentiles who found preaching to be a foolish activity! (1 Cor. 1:21) Still, preaching and teaching have a powerful anointing and blessing from God and ought to be part of what happens in our gatherings. One person talking to the many is modeled and encouraged over seventy times in the New Testament:

> *Jesus* preached and taught continually, from the beginning of His ministry (Mt. 4:17) to the very end (Acts 1:3), even going so far as to say that this is why He had come (Mark 1:38).

The disciples were commissioned by Jesus to preach and teach (Mark 3:14), and they preached everywhere (Mark 16:20).

The early church taught and preached to the lost (Acts 8:4) and to the believers (Acts 14:35). They preached in larger meetings in the public arena and also in the smaller context of home meetings (Acts 20:20). Paul talked so long to the Christians that someone fell asleep and fell out the window (Acts 20:7-11)! He actually spoke through the entire night from dusk to dawn--one person speaking to the many. When in Ephesus, Paul taught the believers day and night for three years (Acts 20:31).

The pastoral epistles of 1 and 2 Timothy, which are highly applicable to every church today, reveal a strong exhortation to publicly read, teach, and preach the Scriptures (1 Tim. 4:13; 2 Tim. 4:2) in church gatherings, even going so far as to say that preaching and teaching is part of the job description of at least some of the elders of the church (1 Tim. 5:17).

The balance of participation and preaching/teaching is one of the challenges we face in having Scriptural gatherings. As we're thinking about gatherings, there is another important factor to consider.

Planned Spontaneity

I have both read of and spoken personally with church leaders who typically plan Sunday services down to the minute. They believe strongly that God has led them to have the kinds of meetings that are orchestrated with excellence, and for them, this means excellent planning. This is especially common in both orthodox, liturgical churches and in seeker-sensitive churches.

I have also read of and spoken personally with church leaders who believe that a meeting has no value and is clearly not led by the Holy Spirit if it is not completely spontaneous. In their minds, to plan for a service is to leave out the Holy Spirit. This is especially true in smaller, independent, Pentecostal and charismatic churches and in renewal churches of any denomination.

Of course, the Bible really teaches both of these perspectives. Proverbs 16:9 is an example of how the Scriptures embrace the dynamic kingdom tension of both of these realities: "In his heart a man plans his course, but the LORD determines his steps." The Living Bible says it even more clearly: "We should make our plans, counting on God to direct us." The alternative to choosing either only planning or only spontaneity is to take the best of each of these mindsets and combine them for great effectiveness. A friend of mine calls it being smart *and* Spirit-filled! I call it "planned spontaneity." Kingdom churches that experience planned spontaneity can enjoy the best of the power of planning and the joy of spontaneity. And this combination of Word and Spirit, or planning and spontaneity, of preaching and participation, is the dream of many in the emerging church.

To that end, let's look at four principles that are especially applicable to those who are leading or facilitating a kingdom gathering:

Spirit-Led Thematic Planning. As the leadership team of a kingdom church seeks God together, we sometimes discern overall themes and seasons that will impact our planning and preparation. Like the pedals on a bicycle, God may be "pushing" on a particular theme or emphasis, such as family, outreach, prophecy, or healing. We can honor Him by leaning into these Spirit-led themes while also allowing room for the Lord to orchestrate the elements of our times together in a way that release His theme. We can set sail for our destination while allowing the wind of the Spirit to determine our exact course to get there.

Prayer First. Regardless of the format or purpose of any meeting, most gatherings in the church in the West are thin in the area of praying about the gathering ahead of time. Every time that we gather ought to have been first bathed in prayer. It is a holy activity to assemble people in the name of the Lord Jesus Christ. Prayer expresses our dependence on God to do what only He can do. The results we are looking for must come from heaven, whether it is a gathering aimed at winning lost people, strengthening the church, or both. "Unless the LORD builds the house, its builders labor in vain." -- Ps. 127:1 As we prepare for gatherings, we are discerning from the Lord the purpose of the gathering. What does *He* want to do? Heart preparation must take precedence over strategic planning. Preparation means that the people who will be leading or facilitating the meeting have gone before God to prepare their hearts, to listen for His instruction, and to wait in His presence. Much of what passes for pre-service prayer in our churches is simply a quick request for God to bless what we are doing. There must be a context where God can speak to us and lead us, in real time, even to the point of speaking to us to lay aside part or all of our agenda and to do something different, even spontaneous. Of course, God's leading can be entirely in the planning stages, and then we simply execute His plan. But even when I have prepared a specific Biblical message that I end up preaching, the prayer before our gatherings has been used by God to influence, fine-tune, and clarify the message God has given me.

Spirit-Led Default Setting. It is important to prayerfully determine among your leadership team what elements you believe God desires in your gatherings. It is not unspiritual to have a default setting for the elements of your gathering. These can include worship, preaching, announcements, offering, ministry, intercession, meals, communion, videos, open sharing, testimonies, etc. Because not every meeting can accomplish every purpose, it is OK, both Biblically and practically, to plan gatherings, as long as there is sensitivity to the leadership of the Holy Spirit during the planning times.

Prayer During. In the midst of any meeting, leaders (and the entire assembled community) must learn the gentle art of sensitivity to the Holy Spirit and flexibility on our feet. This does not come naturally to most people. Why is this essential? Because for Jesus to be Head of the Church, and for the Holy Spirit to truly lead us, we must be subject to the leadership of the Spirit and the Headship of Jesus "on the spot", *in real time.* In other words, God's leading in our lives cannot be relegated to only when we are planning the annual preaching calendar. He must also be Lord of the actual gathering itself. We instruct people to live "moment by moment by Jesus" and to allow the Lord to lead them spontaneously into encounters with lost people in the marketplace. We must practice this same level of spiritual sensitivity to God in our gatherings. In Acts 10, Peter was in a situation where the Lord made him pay attention "on his feet." In the middle of his message to a group of God-seekers, the Holy Spirit fell and interrupted his sermon (Acts 10:44). Peter quickly recognized what was happening and switched gears, turning the meeting into a testimony time and a baptism service (vv. 46, 48). This is the kind of sensitivity needed in our churches and among our leaders.
Jesus instructed us to be willing to leave the ninety-nine to go after the one. I believe this is true even in

our gatherings. There are times where God will ask the many to wait patiently while He diverts His attention on the one. He modeled this all the time.

The Dwelling Place Of God

Ephesians 2:22 tells us that the church is becoming a dwelling place in which God lives by His Spirit. This reference to a corporate dwelling is an invitation from God to His people to create a place where He can dwell in our midst, and because this reference of the church is plural, this involves our gatherings.

> "This is what the LORD says: 'Heaven is my throne, and the earth is my footstool. Where is the house you will build for me? Where will my resting place be?'" --Isa. 66:1

As living stones, the collective body of Christ in a given place and sphere make up the house of the Lord. God is expressing His desire to be with us as a place where He can live and rest. He is looking for people who will create a dwelling place for His Person and His Presence.

This has everything to do with our gatherings. If the first commandment is to have first place, then our gatherings must honor the Person and Presence of God ahead of anything else--not in theory, but in practice. He is church. The Holy Spirit is a gentle Dove, recognizing when our agendas take priority over His Presence. The Person of God must be honored at every single one of our gatherings more than anyone else's person or presence. His Person is our first priority, ahead of even equipping or evangelism.

FACILITATING GATHERINGS

How we conduct meetings has to do with the context of the gatherings. Appropriate meeting "protocol" in one setting may not be the way to do things in another gathering. This is determined largely by our purpose.

What can we learn, then, about facilitating gatherings in kingdom churches that include the best of planning and spontaneity? We close this chapter with 10 applications that summarize how to have gatherings in a more Biblical, powerful way:

1. **We gather best when we've been scattered most.**
   If the culture of the people who are gathering is outward, then the gatherings are that much sweeter.

2. **We don't get hung up on our gathering environment.**
   Jesus gathered people around a stinky fishing boat. Surely it's OK for us to gather in a gymnasium, a living room, a bar, or wherever it works best. Facilities facilitate...period.

3. **We don't get hung up on our gathering size.**
   Let's not fixate on whether the entire Church is supposed to adopt a cell/house church model, or whether megachurches are good or bad. This is shallow thinking. Let's focus on why we're gathering and encountering God and each other. Let's gather big and small and in between, for the sake of a lost world desperately in need of Jesus!

4. **We discern God's purpose of each of our gatherings.**
   Why are we meeting? What are we trying to accomplish? This is key. The rest will fall into place as we understand God's heart and His agenda for our time together.

5. **We come prepared to participate at every gathering.**
   Everyone come as though you will participate--and then do it! Even when there is a main speaker, there are still opportunities to bring our offering and to lean into what God is doing.

6. We expect the Spirit to lead us.
We wait on God before and during our gatherings to discern His direction, because His agenda is always best!

7. We expect the unexpected.
We believe in the creative, spontaneous nature of God to be expressed in the assembly of the saints!

8. We have a track to run on.
Planning is good, not fleshly! God is a planner! Be liberated to hear God during the preparation stage, not just on your feet!

9. We evaluate what we're doing.
We have no sacred cows. We're not afraid to take a hard look at what's working and what's not--and then improve. Even a prophet only sees in part, so we must be learners in process.

10. We bathe every gathering in prayer.
We're more about preparation than planning, because we know that God can do a whole lot more than we can. People are gathering to see Jesus, not us, anyway! So we bathe it in prayer, counting on His leadership, knowing that He loves people more than we do, and He wants to be with us!

Chapter Eight
Kingdom ADVANCEMENT

"What shall we say the kingdom of God is like, or what parable shall we use to describe it? It is like a mustard seed, which is the smallest seed you plant in the ground. Yet when planted, it grows and becomes the largest of all garden plants, with such big branches that the birds of the air can perch in its shade." --Mark 4:30-32

The kingdom of God cannot be stopped! It is expanding throughout the earth at an incredibly rapid rate and it is picking up speed. This is the time for the church to stand up and lift up her head, because our redemption is drawing near (Lk. 21:28). Jesus likened the kingdom to something small in the beginning, such as a mustard seed in Mark 4, or as a little bit of yeast in Matthew 13. Yet, because of the exponential quality of the kingdom, it grows and spreads until it affects everything around it. The kingdom of God, when planted, yields results that are much larger than the way things started. This is why the prophet tells Zechariah not to despise the day of small beginnings. When the kingdom of God is at work, the possibilities are exponential.

One of the great joys of building kingdom churches is that we have the amazing privilege of partnering and co-laboring with the King and with each other as we help expand and multiply His kingdom on earth.

But how does the kingdom of God multiply and expand? What are the factors that cause this advancement to happen? In this chapter I want to look at some of these catalytic factors that release the supernatural reality of kingdom advancement.

In particular, we'll take a look at four kingdom catalysts: (1) Fullness; (2) Diversity; (3) Power; and (4) Multiplication.

FULLNESS

"And you have been given *fullness* in Christ, who is the head over every power and authority." --Col. 2:10

Kingdom churches embrace fullness, and when we build with fullness, we unlock exponential possibility. Having only part of the kingdom, only part of our inheritance, a little bit of unity, a whiff of power, a smidgen of diversity...these things will never do. There is a generation rising that must have fullness! They insist on it, and this is a trait of the people of the kingdom of God.

A mentor and friend of mine likes to say, "I want to build a church that runs on all eight cylinders." I love that! Why settle for a church that is excellent at worship and poor at discipleship? Why embrace a paradigm of church life where we can be prophetic but not evangelistic? Kingdom churches "run on all eight cylinders." This is Biblical and right. Colossians 2:10 tells us that we have been given fullness in Christ. Fullness is our inheritance.

Fullness stretches us and calls us higher. It is easier to walk without fullness (and settle) than to embrace the fullness of the kingdom. The scope and reality of the kingdom is huge, and fullness is Biblical, because it originates in the Person of God.

The Fullness Of God

One of the most captivating prayers in the New Testament is found in Ephesians 3, where Paul describes the content of his intercession for the church in Ephesus. He asks God for strength and power for his friends. He cries out for them to have faith and love and the ability to grasp a fresh revelation of the love of God. And then, in verse 19, he tells us why he is praying these things: "...that you may be filled to the measure of all the fullness of God." The fullness of God! To think that the people of God could be filled with the fullness of His own Person is amazing. In 2 Corinthians 13:14, Paul gives one of my favorite benedictions in the Scriptures: "Now may the grace of our Lord Jesus Christ, the love of God [the Father], and the fellowship of the Holy Spirit, be with you all" (brackets mine). The fullness of God involves the Father's love, the lavish grace of the Bridegroom Jesus, and intimate friendship with the Spirit of God. Some churches focus on the Father and His love. Others focus on the Person of Christ. Still others are all about the Spirit. Kingdom churches embrace the fullness of the Person of God as revealed in Father, Son, and Spirit.

Fullness Of God's Word

In Colossians 1:25, the apostle Paul describes his assignment from God to His Church when he says, "I have become its servant by the commission God gave me to present to you the Word of God *in its fullness.*" Paul was committed to the fullness of God's Word. He essentially declared the same commitment to the church in Ephesus when he told them, "I did not shrink from declaring to you the whole counsel of God" (Acts 20:27). From parenting to praying for the sick, we want to build kingdom churches that declare to people the whole counsel of God. Paul was committed to fullness in his teaching. He understood the dynamic kingdom tension in building a people of the Word and a people of the Spirit. In some churches, only certain topics are "spiritual," while other meat and potatoes subjects are not exciting enough to give attention to. Not so in kingdom churches. They provide a balanced diet with all the nutrients of God's Word. Being radical does not mean being incomplete. Fullness in God's Word is right!

Fullness Of Maturity

We need all of God's people using all of their God-given gifts and serving to all of their God-given potential so that we can all reach a place of maturity that releases the fullness of Christ in our midst.

> "It was he who gave some to be apostles, some to be prophets, some to be evangelists, and some to be pastors and teachers, to prepare God's people for works of service, so that the body of Christ may be built up *until we all* reach unity in the faith and in the knowledge of the Son of God and become mature, *attaining to the whole measure of the fullness of Christ.*" --Eph. 4:11-13

In particular, each of the five gifts listed in Ephesians 4:11 must be operational in kingdom churches in order for us to reach a place of fullness in Christ. This is why we must give heed to the growing cry of the people of God for churches that embrace all aspects of what is called the "five-fold" ministry gifts of Ephesians 4:11. People no longer want to build a church around the primary gift or gifts of the senior pastor. More importantly, it's just not Biblical to do so. It isn't fullness, and it doesn't produce maturity in the people of God. Rather than just a teaching church, or just a prophetic church, or just an outward church, people want it all--and they should! This is how God has 'wired' His people. We can and should want fullness of maturity through the balanced expression of these five equipping gifts.

The text in Ephesians is clear, using "kai" (and) as a means to group these five equipping roles. This means that in order for the body of Christ to experience true fullness of maturity, we must build churches where all five of these gifts—apostle, prophet, evangelist, pastor, teacher—are working together and in the same community to edify and equip the saints. This is God's plan. Ephesians 1:22-23 tells us that the church *is* the fullness of Christ. When the body functions together in fullness, we see a literal, physical expression of the fullness of God.

DIVERSITY

"Once again, the kingdom of heaven is like a net that was let down into the lake and caught *all kinds of fish*."
--Matt. 13:47

The kingdom of God catches all kinds of fish. The Greek word for "caught" here in Matthew 13 is most often rendered "gathered" in the rest of the New Testament. In the book of Acts, in particular, the word *'sunago'* refers to the assembly of the saints. Anyone who has been part of a local church for any length of time knows that the church gathers "all kinds."

Much of the church in the West sees this as a negative truth. The opposite of diversity is uniformity, and frankly, from a management standpoint, churches are easier to 'manage' when uniformity is promoted. A key principle in the church growth movement is the intentional effort to minimize diversity by focusing on homogeneous groupings. Evidently, studies show that churches grow bigger when you weed out the ones that aren't like you.

But this kind of thinking has a big price tag. Wherever the goal of the church is growth rather than the kingdom of God, kingdom diversity will suffer. Over four decades ago, Martin Luther King, Jr. declared eleven o'clock on Sunday mornings to be the most segregated hour in America. The church growth principle of homogeneous grouping hasn't helped change this sad reality. While we enjoy stereotype churches because they're easier to grow, and conforming Christians because they're easier to manage, God has always delighted in diversity.

With the exception of a few notable churches sprinkled here and there that already walk in great diversity, the majority of churches in the West have yet to experience the Biblical tension over God's call to kingdom diversity. We have enjoyed a shallow kind of unity based on conformity, homogeneous groupings, and a vibe of cool and comfortability that suits us. But we're not supposed to be building this thing for us! According to the Lord's prayer in Matthew 6, heaven is meant to touch earth in every aspect of life. God is now calling us to see heaven touch earth in the realm of diversity. The church is meant to reflect heaven, which reflects the heart of God. The kind of church standing before Him in heaven is quite diverse:

> "After this I looked and there before me was a great multitude that no one could count, *from every nation, tribe, people and language,* standing before the throne and in front of the Lamb..." --Rev. 7:9

We know, for example, that here on earth, the animal kingdom separates and groups itself according to its own kind. But the kingdom of heaven displays what is possible under the rule of God. Twice, as Isaiah prophetically describes heaven, he speaks of diversity in the midst of unity: the wolf and the lamb, the leopard and the goat, dwelling together in unity (cf. Isa. 11:6; 65:25).

This diversity in the midst of unity pleases God. Part of the reason I believe God delights in kingdom diversity on earth is because where there is true diversity, Biblical unity is unexplainable except through the power and presence of the Holy Spirit. The outpouring of the Holy Spirit in Acts 2 brought together people from 15 different nations and regions of the Middle East to hear the gospel--people diverse in ethnicity, language, and culture. Undoubtedly, some of those 3,000 people who joined the church in a day were made up of from among this diverse crowd of people.

But we mustn't assume that the heart of kingdom diversity is achieved when we have people from a variety of racial backgrounds attending our services. In some places, this just isn't feasible, because the ethnicity of the geography means that the church will draw from a uniform demographic. In fact, a church can be made up of people from mostly the same racial and socioeconomic backgrounds and still embrace and practice kingdom diversity. While I believe we must continue to break down racial and socioeconomic walls in order to experience diversity in these realms, this is not the only way to model diversity. There are other dimensions of kingdom diversity that every church can embrace, wherever they are in the West, regardless of the ethnicity of their geography.

Recognizing and embracing our differences is essential in order for us to depart from "one size fits all" church life and discipleship strategy and flow in diversity. Program-based design churches tend to count on uniformity, while kingdom churches are good with God's "blended family." [Contrary to a growing cry in the church in the West, programs are not evil. A program is defined as "a formulated plan listing things to be done." God was involved in 'program' during the creation of the world, when he planned with wisdom each step of the way (Prov. 8:27-31).] To embrace a revival atmosphere that causes growth in every believer, and not just in the homogeneous group in the middle, kingdom diversity is our essential backdrop.

Intergenerational Mentoring

God designed the church as a family. It is not simply *like* a family; it *is* a family. As such, we can greatly benefit from intergenerational mentoring that comes through one-on-one discipling relationships.

Deep within each of us is a God-given need to love and to be loved, to feel significant in our impact upon others, while at the same time allowing others into our lives to help us grow and become all we are called to become in Jesus Christ. This need can be addressed in mentoring relationships. Mentoring relationships occur in all 'directions.' There are those relationships where we are being mentored by someone else. There are those relationships where we are actively mentoring another person or small group of people. Finally, there are those relationships where each person

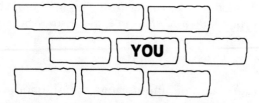

'mentors' the other in a peer-level way. We need all types of relationships in our lives in an ongoing way, much like the stones in a wall are surrounded by those stones above, to either side, and below. When we "mentor" someone else, we are helping that person become a disciple of Jesus. We are pouring ourselves into them, teaching them what we know, and holding them accountable in their desire to become more like their Master. When we see success in our efforts and genuine growth occur, we are like "proud parents." When we have peer-level mentoring relationships, we mutually benefit, as Proverbs 27:17 indicates: "As iron sharpens iron, so one man sharpens another." We also need the other kind of mentoring relationships where we receive spiritual help, input, and accountability from a caring person who has something to offer us.

Fathers And Mothers

Far more is caught than taught, and building an intergenerational church full of *models* is a worthy kingdom goal. People in kingdom churches will rise to the call to live lives worthy of imitation. Paul boldly said, "Follow my example, as I follow the example of Christ" (1 Cor. 11:1). But did you know that at one point, Paul even went so far as to tell people just to imitate him? Listen to the bold exhortation coming from a mature veteran in the faith to a church struggling with basic maturity issues:

> "Even though you have ten thousand guardians in Christ, you do not have many fathers, for in Christ Jesus I became your father through the gospel. Therefore *I urge you to imitate me.* For this reason I am sending to you Timothy,

my son whom I love, who is faithful in the Lord. He will remind you of *my way of life* in Christ Jesus, which agrees with what I teach everywhere in every church." --1 Cor. 4:15-17

This intergenerational mentoring is not gender-specific. Aquila and Priscilla, a husband-wife team, pulled Apollos aside and mentored him in his understanding of the gospel (18:26). Paul referred to himself as both a spiritual father and a spiritual mother to the Thessalonians (1 Thess. 2:6-12).

Part of the apostolic reformation that is occurring in our day has to do with the love of our Father God flowing through us to one another. God is truly turning the hearts of His people back to a proper apostolic fathering dynamic that will be healthy and appropriate, free from control but with great love that finally removes the orphan spirit from the church in the West and causes us to cry and call out, "Papa! Papa! I am loved by my Father!" (cf. Rom. 8:15; Gal. 4:6).

Walking as fathers and sons is always first and foremost a heart issue. It requires a prophetic work of God to turn our hearts toward fathers and sons. We need to ask God for a heart revelation so we can trust again (Mal. 4:1-6). This revelation comes not only through spiritual encounters but through loving human examples of fatherhood and sonship in our lives.

Becoming A Spiritual Father. A spiritual father (non-gender) is all about helping those in his sphere of influence to reach their God-given potential, to fulfill their destiny, and to finish well. Spiritual parents not only display the characteristics of basic spiritual maturity and victory, but they know God in a way that makes others hungry. Spiritual fathers spend time with children, modeling life. They encourage their children by calling out potential and destiny. They are not passive but take the lead in the relationship, fighting for their children, jealous for their success. A father makes reasonable demands on his children, calling them higher and to a place of excellence. He is not afraid to bring needed correction but is also ready to forgive. When a father doesn't know something, he freely admits his own weaknesses and walks in the freedom of personal vulnerability. He accepts misunderstanding as part of the cost of fathering and pushes past it for the well-being of his sons.

Becoming A Spiritual Son. Tired of dominant leaders, many Christians misuse the verse where Jesus says not to call any man on earth "father" (Mt. 23:9). In this same passage, Jesus says not to call anyone on earth "teacher." But Ephesians 4:11 plainly tells us that there are teachers in the body of Christ, and Paul the Apostle, under the inspiration of the Spirit, calls himself a teacher on at least two occasions (1 Tim. 2:7; 2 Tim. 1:11). Is Paul in violation of Jesus' warning? I don't think so. Jesus was addressing the motive of the heart. He was denouncing the pharisaical use of titles, not the proper use of words to describe Biblical functions. In the same way, Paul called himself a father and others he called 'sons.' This is good and right, because it describes not a title given from a false motive, but rather a functional relationship that gives life.

A spiritual son (or daughter) is someone who willingly receives life and help from a spiritual father or mother. It is important that we understand our need to be both fathers/mothers and sons/daughters. When we are younger, both in age and in the Lord, we can have many spiritual "parents" who will provide a mentoring role in our lives, but we are spiritual fathers to few or none. This is good and right! The need for such mentoring is much greater than when we are seasoned, mature, and occupying a significant fathering role ourselves.

The Apostle John describes a progression in the faith where one becomes a "father" in the faith, and the implication is that the role of being a "son" is no longer his primary role (1 John 2:12-14). It is doubtful that the Apostle Paul had a spiritual father in his life toward his latter years, or that the Apostle John, on the Isle of Patmos, was a spiritual "son" to anyone, although he carried that heart. Still, it is best, when it can happen, that we all, at whatever age, receive mentoring, fathering, and mothering, from significant people in our lives. Whether we are receiving from a spiritual father or mother or not, there are heart attitudes within sons and daughters that we need to cultivate--what the Bible calls the "spirit of sonship" (Rom. 8:15) rather than the spirit of slavery/servitude.

One way to discern the heart and activity of sons is to contrast them with mere servants. Sons are faithful to build the house while servants are looking to build a ministry. Sons put the family first and use the language of "we", while servants put issues first. Sons inherit, therefore they feel ownership and responsibility, while servants take, seeking their own. Sons honor and protect authority, while servants continually challenge authority because they feel that they know better. It's not wrong to question, and truth is valued in healthy families, but sons are secure and can submit in a healthy way. Sons allow love to cover a multitude of sins, while servants expose weakness. Sons delight in their fathers and rally people to them, while servants rally people to themselves. Sons have puppy feet and are teachable, while servants come full-grown, trying to teach everyone what they know. Servants are defensive because they are afraid of rejection, but sons are correctable because they are secure in their father's love.

Diversity And Mentoring

Kingdom diversity is preserved best when we honor the intergenerational dynamic of Biblical family. This dynamic allows mentoring relationships throughout the church, whether aided by the structure of a formal discipleship system or simply encouraged and celebrated as they occur naturally. Either way, mentoring relationships of spiritual fathering and sonship provide the Lord an opportunity for divine 'matchmaking', where God uses the one to strengthen the other.

Customized Growth

Another dimension of kingdom diversity is customized growth. When I was a public school teacher, I taught "all kinds" of students. While on the one hand I enjoyed the diversity, for the ease of teaching I also really enjoyed having the class "on the same page." I would design lesson plans that aimed at the middle. I realized there were advanced students in my classes, and I tried to give them some advanced work to do. I was also aware of other students who required extra attention and assistance to complete their assignments. But in terms of learning, because of the constraints of time, staffing, curriculum, and evaluations, I was forced to design learning systems that captured the majority of my students. Conformity and uniformity were essential to survival!

Somewhere in the back of my mind, I was aware of certain "special" schools where learning was more customized, but I knew there was no way that would work in my school system. In order for me to truly customize the method and materials by which each student learned, we would have to embrace an entirely different learning philosophy. We would have to measure school success differently. Our classroom would have to be arranged differently, and many more teachers would have to be involved with my students. Teachers of other subjects would have to agree to this system, and the entire school and district would have to make a major paradigm shift in principles and practice.

Customizing learning isn't just limited to how we conduct classroom activity. Not too many years ago, home schooling was unheard of and looked at with suspicion and disdain. By contrast, recently I was sitting next to a seven-year old boy with a Sony VIAO laptop who was doing his school work from a set of DVDs while his mother checked in and oversaw his progress. Due to work requirements, this family enjoys a very mobile lifestyle. A customized learning process for this young boy is essential so that he can get a proper education.

Customization, mobilization, personalization, and hands-on participation are all related trends that represent a cultural megashift in the society of the West. In addition to changes in education, the corporate world is adapting as well. Companies and organizations are creating new ways to work and job share, expanding their definitions of the office, with some employees working thousands of miles from their corporate headquarters. Retail stores like Home Depot have experienced explosive growth because of the trend towards "do-it-yourself" thinking and lifestyles. The world wide web is the ultimate tool in leveling the playing field for an informed, hands-on way to access information and to achieve personal growth and development.

This kind of "out-of-the-box" thinking toward customization is revolutionizing the mindset and practice of our Western society. But what about the church? Again, I do not believe the church should cater to the culture. However, because diversity is a kingdom reality, that means God thought of it first! And if it takes the culture to remind us of the truth, then so be it. Because growth is the goal of so many churches, aiming for the middle becomes second nature. Standardization becomes an unconscious way of thinking, and there is little room for creativity outside programs.

Kingdom churches understand and embrace the unique call each person has that is part of them. Since the center of their paradigm is not the church but Jesus and his kingdom, the individual is more important than the institution, and therefore creating means for growth for each person are vital. Creativity of ministry expression is celebrated and cultivated.

Intentional Discipleship

We can celebrate diversity while still being intentional about our discipleship process. Most healthy, growing churches have an intentional plan for helping to produce Christ followers. These plans may be expressed any number of ways. Many churches have asked people to attend a series of discipleship classes. Other churches have opted for a more personalized growth paradigm where mentors meet with individuals and in small cells, going through written materials. Still others utilize discipleship events, such as weekends away, to provide catalytic moments of focus on certain aspects of discipleship and growth. Our local church is taking the best of these approaches and developing a hybrid "intentional discipleship pathway" that helps provide a track to run on.

It is important, though, in the midst of whatever plan we develop, that we understand the mosaic nature of people's learning processes. In the past, we have been purely linear in our thinking. We have envisioned a world where people only learn one way and only in one sequence. This is what creates a rigid, programmatic system that may work well in some more uniform cultures but which has more difficulty in our Western culture. People learn through various means.

We can be intentional about the discipleship process without taking on the role of God and forcing people to "grow" according to our program.

Personal Development Plans

It is the destiny of the church to serve God by advancing His kingdom. We are priests, every one of us, called by God to advance His kingdom personally and collectively. At our local church, we are working on 'Personal Development Plans' for every person. We want individuals to customize their own growth through a focused life with God-given priorities and goals at every given season of life. These plans help honor kingdom diversity and strengthen the idea that we are about helping each person succeed in fulfilling their God-given destiny, rather than simply trying to fill slots within the institution of the church. Personal Development Plans have been helpful to customize the discipleship process for individuals. They provide the balance to the classes and weekends we hold that are more uniform in nature.

All of these processes are accomplished in the context of mentoring relationships, which is what keeps things flexible, customized, and personal.

KINGDOM POWER

"For the kingdom of God is not a matter of talk but of power." --1 Cor. 4:20

For kingdom advancement to occur in any significant way, power is required and is not optional. Kingdom churches are filled with the reality and demonstration of the power of God. This verse in 1 Corinthians represents the striking reality that the very essence and nature of God's kingdom is power. It is complimentary to Romans 1:16, where Paul proclaims that the gospel is the power of God to salvation for everyone who believes. Clearly, Paul is not talking about a gospel of mere words. The gospel of words has power, but the kingdom doesn't come through talking heads. Raw power is part and parcel with the gospel. Anything less is Biblically suspect and is to be avoided:

"There will be *terrible* times in the last days. People will be lovers of themselves...lovers of pleasure rather than lovers of God--*having a form of godliness but denying its power.* Have nothing to do with them." --2 Tim. 3:1-5

Surveying the landscape of churches in the West, it is clear that many church leaders have been holding onto a worldview of power as optional, or worse yet, as something that is suspect. All too often our greatest strengths become our greatest weaknesses. Because God's power is dynamic, unpredictable, and sometimes even 'messy', those who work the hardest to be Biblically accurate and theologically sound are often the worst offenders at ignoring and avoiding the Biblical reality of the power of God. In short, we have been trying to build New Testament churches marked by kingdom reality without New Testament power. The lack of power in the church in the West has become embarrassingly obvious.

When I became a Christian in the seventies, I was told by my mentors that God wasn't in the "power" business any more. Demonstrations of God's power were theologically relegated to the validation of Jesus' ministry and to the first thirty years of the early church. After that, I was told, we had God's written Word, and there was no longer a need for supernatural displays of God's power. When I offered examples of people I knew or had heard of who were recently healed of diseases, I was summarily corrected that either (a) the people weren't really sick to begin with; (b) it was a fluke and we shouldn't expect such things; or (c) something other than God's power had healed them--usually medicine, coincidence, or even the devil (which made no sense). As I grew in my Christian faith, studied God's Word more, had more experiences with God's power, and prayed more effective prayers for others, I noticed that my power-challenged friends had a more difficult time defending their position of powerlessness. As communication and testimonies have become more globalized through the internet and better travel, this position of powerlessness is becoming all but indefensible. It was only later that I would realize that this worldview is entirely unbiblical. Power is part and parcel of the nature and activity of kingdom people and kingdom churches.

It is alarming that a still significant (but shrinking) part of the North American church doesn't make room in their theology for the power of God as normative. But what is more alarming is the stunning absence of power in churches that *do* embrace a theology of the supernatural! Over recent decades, we have been able to bluff our way through with only a tacit nod towards power, but now, the power of God flowing through His people in China, South America, Africa, and other places is providing an 'in-your-face' mirror to His people in the West. It is time to build kingdom churches unashamedly filled with the power of God!

Radical Dependency

People in kingdom churches exhibit a total commitment to being continually filled with the Holy Spirit. Many older Christians wistfully remember that when they were new believers, they would just "follow the Spirit!" This is where many great stories came from--those early years of following God. Somewhere, many of us tried to grow up, and we forgot about the childlike essence of the kingdom. This new generation of churches and leaders are exhibiting a radical dependency on the Holy Spirit. *"Immerse me, Spirit of God! Fully possess me, precious Holy Spirit!"* are the kinds of prayers being prayed today by a people absolutely convinced that whatever we do and say and build and plant must be authored, birthed, led, protected, and sealed by the wonderful Spirit of God! These ones, fully committed to the written Word of God as their foundation, realize that it is possible to diligently study the Scriptures and miss the Person of Jesus, just like the pharisees did (Jn. 5:39). We must radically depend on the Holy Spirit.

The Stigma Of Power

How many churches in the West are ashamed of what the Holy Spirit may do when He touches people? How many churches in the West, seeking to be respectable, have grown uneasy with and ashamed of God's power demonstrated in regular (and unusual) ways in and through people? We hedge our bets, we qualify Him, we make excuses for God, and we explain away any demonstrations of power. Rather than shy away from power, the apostolic nature of kingdom churches expects demonstrations of power as *normative*:

> "My message and my preaching were not with wise and persuasive words, but with a *demonstration of the Spirit's power*, so that your faith might not rest on men's wisdom, but *on God's power*." --1 Cor. 2:4-5

As incredible as it may seem, Paul teaches us here to rest our faith *on God's power.* That makes power pretty important. Notice that Paul establishes the causal relationship between kingdom power and the Holy Spirit when he calls it "the Spirit's power."

The Power Of The Gospel

The causal link between the Holy Spirit and power was previously made by Jesus when He said in Acts 1:8--"You shall receive power when the Holy Spirit has come upon you..." It is the Holy Spirit that releases the Divine reality of the power of God. This power allows us to truly be witnesses of an evidential Christianity, a God who is alive and not dead, who is active and not passive, who is passionate towards humanity and not listless, bored, or disinterested. Jesus came out of the desert, a time of temptation and testing, full of the power of the Spirit. He was ready for action because of the power of the Holy Spirit. We, too, must be completely filled with the Spirit and His power to impact a world for Jesus Christ, armed with the Word and the Spirit.

The Glory Of God

In the Old Testament, there were frequent occurrences of the weighty glory of God descending on the people and their gatherings like a thick blanket. To think that because we are under the New Covenant we would not experience this is backwards thinking. How much more, now that we have the indwelling Holy Spirit should our gatherings be characterized by the manifest Presence and Glory of God! 2 Corinthians 3 tells us that we behold God's glory with unveiled faces. The apostle Paul tells us in Ephesians 2:22 that we, the people of God, are being built together to become a dwelling place of God in the Spirit. This means that it is God's intention to live among us and to demonstrate His powerful presence and His beautiful nature in our midst. May the weighty glory of God fill our homes, our cell groups, our house churches, our celebrations, our prayer meetings, and every place where two or three are together. He is in our midst!

KINGDOM MULTIPLICATION

"Give, and it will be given to you. A good measure, pressed down, shaken together and running over, will be poured into your lap. For with the measure you use, it will be measured to you." --Lk. 6:38

One of the primary reasons the Western church has lost its surprise, spontaneity, and power is because of our propensity to measure everything. We count people, dollars, empty chairs, full chairs, small groups, parking spaces, minutes on the clock, graduates from our programs, and so on. In Luke 6:38, Jesus tells us that our measurements will come back to us, one way or another. The law of measurement is this: whatever measurement we use will be measured to us. This is both a promise and a warning.

It's not exactly the actual numbering of things that is the problem (although sometimes it is, as in the case of David numbering Israel). I can already hear the arguments of wise stewards proclaiming loudly that we're just being responsible with what God is giving us. Yes, stewardship is a real responsibility before God. Certainly we must balance our checkbooks, plan wisely for enough space for meetings, and so on. But the heart reality of kingdom measurements has to do with the fact that the kingdom is so incredibly powerful and explosive, it cannot be encompassed by mere human observation and recording.

"The kingdom of God does not come with your careful observation, nor will people say, 'Here it is,' or 'There it is,' because the kingdom of God is within you."
--Lk. 17:20-21

For years we have trained our pastors, church planters, and leadership teams to count everything in sight as part of good stewardship. But I think we've missed a key principle that can significantly limit our thinking and reduce our experience. God wants to take us beyond measurements!

"Now to him who is able to do *immeasurably* more than all we ask or imagine, according to his power that is at work within us" --Eph. 3:20

God is able, but are we able to embrace the infinite ability of God? If He can do more than we could ask in our most fervent prayer times or imagine in our most liberated times of daydreaming, then we are only limited by our current measurements. Truly, we are measured, and therefore we receive, according to the measurements that we use. If we build churches around our common understanding of measurements, then ultimately, we will never know the raw power and potential of God working within us and through us. The term "immeasurably" can be defined as "incapable of being measured; broadly: indefinitely extensive." The intense burden that has been on the leadership of the church in the West will finally be lifted as we understand and are liberated by kingdom measurements into a multiplication mentality.

The Power Of Multiplication

The power of multiplication is a dynamic reality that we experience as we build His kingdom. In Leviticus 26:8, God promised multiplication when He told His people: "Five of you will chase a hundred, and a hundred of you will chase ten thousand..." This spontaneous dynamic of the rapidly expanding kingdom was lived out in the early church on numerous occasions as the church rallied together. For example, after the apostles and the congregation came together to commission seven men to oversee the food ministry, there were immediate results:

"And the word of God increased; and the number of disciples *multiplied...*" --Acts 6:7 (KJV)

God can grow things through addition or through multiplication. Because we are living in the eleventh hour before the return of Christ, and because we want to redeem the time before us, kingdom churches are focused on multiplication, not simply addition. Addition occurs as we each do our part, but multiplication happens when we come together.

Through Unity. Kingdom churches love the whole church. They have made a decision to avoid self-preservation, which leads to comparison, envy, hoarding, and competition. Instead, kingdom churches believe that the kingdom truly does come first. With a kingdom orientation, there is nothing to gain and nothing to lose. There cannot be competition, because there is nothing to compete over. We genuinely want other individuals and churches to succeed.

This heart of unity allows us to embrace one another without sizing each other up. Jesus' prayer will be answered! There will be unity. The only question is whether or not we will be included or replaced. Lest you think that statement is harsh, remember what happened to the unbelieving Israelites when they wouldn't go into the promised land. God *replaced* them, *every single one,* with a brand new generation of people who would obey Him. God is currently replacing leaders who will not embrace the call to unity. He is raising up new leaders and building new churches that will truly embrace unity, even at their own expense. It is foolish to think that only some will pay a price. *Everyone* pays a price for unity. Everyone has to die to at least some aspect of their dreams and plans for true unity to take place. But wherever unity truly happens, it releases incredible multiplying power.

Through Partnership. Loving the whole church is a good beginning, but God is causing apostolic networks and city/regional ministry partnerships to emerge. We will see more and more churches and their leaders begin to come together in order to actually *build* together. The planting of houses of prayer in cities and regions is an example of how God is rallying people around regional ministries that are generally larger than any single church. Churches are also beginning to partner as apostolic networks are forming. These networks will replace denominations in significance and impact as God brings forth apostolic leadership in this hour.

Through Sending. Multiplication also occurs through sending! When we give away our best to seed the nations of the earth and in particular to reach the poor of the earth, our kingdom impact is exponentially increased, and God is well-pleased.

> "And this gospel *of the kingdom* will be preached in the whole world as a testimony to all nations, and then the end will come." --Matt. 24:14

Though we haven't talked much about it in this book, sending must absolutely include the poor of the earth as central to our mission. My favorite book to explain this compelling heart for the poor is Always Enough by Rolland and Heidi Baker, which I highly recommend to every kingdom church builder. Loving the poor is not optional in kingdom churches, and the Bakers embody the kind of heart and practice that every kingdom church gladly and humbly embraces. Advancing the kingdom means bringing good news to the poor, both spiritually and physically.

Despise Not Small Beginnings

Jesus' prayer for unity will be answered, and the labor we are doing is not in vain! Small efforts yield big results when they are based in the kingdom of God.

> "What shall we say the kingdom of God is like, or what parable shall we use to describe it? It is like a mustard seed, which is the smallest seed you plant in the ground. Yet when planted, it grows and becomes the largest of all garden plants, with such big branches that the birds of the air can perch in its shade." --Mark 4:30-32

I want to encourage those of you who strongly desire to see the church come together in your city or region. Your desire originates in God's heart, so don't lose heart! When you fight for unity, you are entering into the perfect will of God. The dream in the heart of Jesus for unity expressed in John 17 will be answered, and therefore when you dream the dreams of God, you will see fulfillment! He identifies with and appreciates your desire for unity, and He will bless your efforts. May the Lord Himself grant you favor as you build the kingdom in your sphere!

Epilogue
Kingdom CULTURE

"One day as he was teaching...the power of the Lord was present for him to heal the sick...and the people all tried to touch him, because power was coming from him and healing them all." --Luke 5:17 & 6:19

We hope this book will serve those building kingdom churches. As much as we have tried to be clear and helpful for the sake of those involved in the building process, a lot of what we have been describing in this book is not able to be captured and quantified in a prescriptive, programmatic way. It is about heart, about atmosphere, about lifestyle, about perspective, and about culture. The atmosphere of a people, and the heart, culture, and paradigm from which they operate, are far more influential than the church calendar or strategy sessions or any other thing.

It is the same mystery that operates when two equal athletes, each properly fed and trained and groomed, do not run in the same way. All other things being equal, often one will excel because of sheer heart. Kingdom churches may not have everything "down," but they excel because the posture of the hearts of a like-minded people is in tune with Christ's kingdom.

When Jesus ministered, the atmosphere was pregnant with power and promise. This is why everyone tried to touch Him. They sensed something different. They felt the possibilities when they were around Him. The impossible looked much more attainable in His presence. Their dreams didn't feel foolish anymore. *They* didn't feel foolish anymore.

In fact, they began to forget about themselves. They were captivated by Another.

Kingdom churches are pregnant with power and promise because Jesus is walking in their midst. He still creates an atmosphere of surprise and anticipation wherever He is. It's not about a location, because Jesus will dwell with and walk in the midst of any people who seek first His kingdom and righteousness, regardless of where and how often they meet.

The culture of the kingdom produces powerful impact in a variety of ways. Here are some miscellaneous things I see arising and coming to the church in the West in an increased way as the culture of the kingdom begins to define these churches in the years to come before Christ's return:

A Friend To The Poor

When we planted the church in the Mid-West, we agreed to practice a model of "seek, soak, and go!" We would gather on Sunday mornings, pray for one another and "soak" one another in God's presence and power. Then we would break into teams and go to the projects. We took church to the poor, ministering love and hope to the hearts and practical needs of God's 'chosen' people (cf. James 2:5). When we moved back to the Central Coast of California, we were greatly concerned, because we knew that the "poor" in our geography were not prevalent, and yet ministry to the poor was so central to our mission and heart. My friend David Van Cronkhite says, "We need the poor more than they need us." This is true! Now, in our geography of abundance, we are finding new ways to serve the poor. A large part of our vision is to become an apostolic center helping resource effective ministries to the poor. Serving the poor is not an optional ministry. It is central to our mission (Luke 4:18) and central to what it means to know God (Jer. 22:15-16). God is turning the attention of the church in the West on the plight of the poor. Even movie stars are jumping on the bandwagon. Pure religion! Let it come to us in the West.

Presence Evangelism

The light shines brighter as darkness increases! As we walk in the presence of the King, those who don't know Christ experience God's presence and respond. We will see more and more people coming to Christ as the people of God exude the holiness of our King. As the church begins to embody the kingdom and become again living epistles known and read by all men, as believers begin to "outlive" their unbelieving contemporaries, the contrast between those who know God and those who don't will again become evident. There will also be increased supernatural expressions of healing, words of knowledge, prophecies, miracles, and signs and wonders released in the marketplace as believers walk in the presence and power of God and begin to take risks again for the sake of the King. Many more people will come to Christ as they see and experience an evidential Christianity and a God who is clearly alive and present in a holy, mobilized people.

Prodigals Returning

There are thousands of believers who have come to know Christ but have abandoned the church. Now is the time for these ones to reestablish fellowship with a local body of believers. The last decade of deconstruction that caused many believers to grow disillusioned with the church is over! God allowed thousands of us to see what is wrong so that the dismantling of the ship called the church in Acts 27 would take place. But read the story. Paul said, "Unless these men stay with the ship, you cannot be saved." This is not the time to jump ship on the church. Only if we all stay on the ship together and go through the process together, first of deconstruction, and now of reconstruction, can everyone live. While the ship of institutionalism is being run aground and destroyed, we are all meant to grab hold of our piece of the ship and go safely to shore. There is safety in going through this transition *with* the people of God, not away from them.

This is not the time to hide in the cave like Elijah, thinking we're the only ones! God has been doing a major, global work in the church in the West. Now, God is building new kinds of churches with new kinds of leaders, and He is refitting existing churches and leaders with a fresh kingdom paradigm. The net result is that the church is becoming safe again. The Father's heart is being released in an increased way so that a generation can come to Christ and so many prodigals can find their way home. When Joseph fled to Egypt to protect Mary and Jesus, the Lord spoke to him at the right time that it was safe to return. In the same way, the Father is saying to many that it is "safe" to return to fellowship with the local body of Christ. Those who remain prodigal after this window of grace will have more difficulty returning and are in danger of hardening their hearts.

The Canopy Of David

Among other things, David's tabernacle (or tent) was characterized by a stunning absence of the veil around the holy of holies. This powerful prophetic picture speaks to us of an intimacy with God available to every believer. When Jesus died on the Cross and the veil of His flesh was torn, so was the veil in the temple. We have unrestricted access, both as individual believers and as a corporate temple of the Lord, to the most intimate places in God available on earth. The promise of the restoration of the tabernacle of David is about this radical intimacy expressed through wholehearted, extravagant worshippers. Over recent years, we have identified with many metaphors as the Church--house, hospital, school, army, etc. But the Bridal metaphor will take highest prominence. As the church finds her identity as the Bride of Christ, intimacy with God will then lead to increased fruitfulness on earth. This radical shift of attention from works to the Person of Jesus changes everything. The Ephesian church that received correction from Jesus in Revelation 2 was working very hard and holding the line on doctrinal purity. But somehow, they had left their first love.

There is a strong bridal call being issued forth from the heart of Jesus Christ to His Church. We will continue to become a people who are confident in God's love for us and His gracious friendship. Each believer will become a literal "house of prayer" on the earth!

The Power Of Love

Many waters cannot quench love, because love is stronger than death. Nothing can separate us from God's love. God's love is the most powerful reality in the universe. Kingdom churches build through the culture of God's love. One church I know has declared the following mission statement: *"That we may walk in God's love and then give it away."* Love will always find a way. We will see arguments solved and tensions reduced by love. Love settles arguments! *When we don't know the way forward, we must call out to God for more love.* The increased love of God is the answer to our challenges as we move forward to build kingdom churches together. Jesus prophesied that in the last days, the love of many would grow cold. Love will be the defining characteristic of true kingdom churches. The love of God will become more prominent because it will grow so thin outside of the kingdom. As darkness increases, the culture of God's love will shine brighter and brighter from God's people.

An Atmosphere Of Possibilities

In the years to come, *encouragement will become a more and more important ministry.* Everyone is carrying around two buckets--one with gas and one with water. We will learn when to pour from which bucket. God has put little fires in people's hearts. It was said of Jesus, "A smoldering wick he will not snuff out." In the same way, the church will become more skilled at calling forth destiny in one another. This atmosphere of grace will empower the church to live out of her true identity. The palette of creativity will emerge even more as individual believers begin to express their love for

God in more spontaneous and creative ways. New sounds in worship will emerge. New kinds of churches will be birthed. Church without walls means that the wineskin of the church will truly be simple, flexible, and supple in the hands of the Master. We will be blown away by the creativity coming through the body of Christ, and the net result will not simply be self-expression, but a tidal wave of people coming to the Lord Jesus Christ. It will be impossible to orchestrate and barely able to be chronicled. Like a river, our choice will be to watch or jump in.

Beyond Structure

Currently, many Western churches are still scrambling for the latest and greatest gathering methodology. But how we gather is really not a wineskin. As of the writing of this book, Sunday morning meetings may still be quite central in many churches while becoming a bit passe with some, and the movements of G12 and house churches are "hot." But look out! God is still using all kinds of contexts! Many of our African brothers and sisters are gathering mostly in relatively large meetings and sitting in rows on the ground or in chairs while one person does the speaking. Traditional Bible schools, crusades, and platform ministry are still popular. The techniques, structures, and gathering contexts they use are not keeping the dead from being raised, blind eyes from opening, food being multiplied, and *thousands from coming into the kingdom*! As this revolution grows, we will find that many have been barking up the wrong tree! How we gather is really actually not a wineskin. It is a context. *The new wineskin is the paradigm and culture of the kingdom, and the wine is extravagant devotion to a Person and the wine of His love in our hearts and lives and families.* A kingdom revolution among a people in love with their King compelled to go to the lost--that's it!

A Prepared Bride

Intimacy with God produces urgency among God's people. We will see an intensity and fervency among these kingdom priests who live everyday as walking revival. A forerunner spirit will emerge as Christ's return hastens and people prepare themselves for the wedding feast of the Lamb. The return of Christ will begin to occupy the thoughts of most believers much more often than is the case today. The Spirit and the Bride will truly say, "Come quickly, Lord Jesus!"

Revolution!

A nameless, faceless generation will emerge, not because of the abolishing of leadership, as many have thought, but because everyone else will "step up." When there are so many living radically for Christ and serving Him with all their hearts, and as kingdom churches deemphasize title and position and focus on function and commonality in Christ, it will be hard to tell who the "leaders" are, except by the fruit of their lives and their kingdom impact. Even then, it won't really matter, because the entire body will have reached a place of maturity, expressing the fullness of the measure of Christ in their stature. We will see the priesthood of every believer in our lifetime. And we will see this priesthood expressing themselves in like-minded communities called "kingdom churches." And it will be glorious.

About The Author

Mark Perry has been a Christian since 1977 and has been actively building kingdom churches since 1991.

Mark has planted or helped plant several churches and has been part of six different church staffs, as assistant pastor, senior pastor, and church consultant.

Mark is currently lead strategist of Everyday Church and regional director of the Central Coast House Of Prayer.

Mark has been married for 19 years and has three daughters.

You can email Mark with questions, comments, and speaking requests at mark@everydaychurch.org.

CPSIA information can be obtained at www.ICGtesting.com
Printed in the USA
LVOW072243040112

262488LV00001B/184/A